STRONG DOCTRINE, STRONG MERCY

Strong doctrine, strong mercy

*a salvationist looks at some major moral
questions of the late 20th century*

by

Shaw Clifton

International Headquarters of The Salvation Army
101 Queen Victoria Street, London EC4P 4EP

Copyright © 1985 The General of The Salvation Army
First published 1985
ISBN 0 85412 471 3

CAPTAIN SHAW CLIFTON

was commissioned as an officer in 1973 with his wife, Helen, following an early career as a lecturer in law at the Inns of Court, London, and at the University of Bristol, Faculty of Law. The captain holds the degrees of Bachelor of Laws and Bachelor of Divinity, and is an Associate of King's College, London.

Captain and Mrs Clifton have served in the British Territory in corps appointments and in Zimbabwe in educational and corps work. The captain is now the Legal Secretary at International Headquarters, London. He is joint editor, with his wife, of the book *Growing Together*.

Cover art work by Jim Moss

Printed in Great Britain by
The Campfield Press, St Albans

CONTENTS

INTRODUCTION

SOME of the material in this book first appeared in 1975 in *The Officer* magazine and was eventually published in booklet form with the title: *What does the salvationist say...?* That material has been updated and included here with much that was published in article form in *The Officer* in 1978 and 1983.

The topics have been chosen because they are currently being given a healthy airing in both religious and secular circles. It is hoped that the book will aid understanding of some of the moral issues facing us today and that readers will be encouraged to shape Christian attitudes (not necessarily identical with those of the writer) for themselves which will stand up to secular challenge.

Finally, and most important of all, with regard to those topics impinging on personal morality, the aim has been to show that what marks out the salvationist's approach to ethics is the application of the two-edged tool of 'strong doctrine with strong mercy'.

Shaw Clifton

1

Marriage and divorce (1)

FOR as long as there have been marriages, there have been failed marriages. We are constantly reminded of the inexorable rise in the divorce rate, and so it does no harm at all to tell ourselves again that in fact happy and successful marriages outnumber those that eventually break down. It is all too easy to believe that marriage is a fading part of our social traditions. It may be true that more is heard nowadays of criticism dubbing marriage outmoded or emotionally inhibiting, but the plain truth is that in many lands marriage is as popular as ever.

For example, in 1982 in the United Kingdom, the Study Commission on the Family published the results of a number of surveys in *Values and the Changing Family*. The Commission concluded that marriage in the UK is alive and well. 'Some 90 per cent of people get married and . . . this is likely to be the trend for the foreseeable future. It would certainly be wrong to assume too readily that divorce suggests a widespread disillusion with marriage itself; for again, many of the divorced get remarried. . . . Moreover, it is arguably the case that divorce often signifies not so much a rejection of marriage but rather a search for a more fulfilling marriage.' This is confirmed by Dr Jack Dominion: 'There is certainly no evidence that there is any serious alternative to marriage which is replacing it' (*Marriage in Britain*, Study Commission on the Family, 1982). In one survey conducted in 1979/80 in Colchester, Essex, a majority of those polled saw marriage and family life as the most important aspect of their lives. Marriage and family were consistently ranked ahead of health, job, money or friends.

Similar good news comes from the USA. The American *War Cry* for 8 January 1983 carried a review of *Reaffirmation: Renewing Your Marriage Vows and Values* by Sandra Carter (Harmony Books) which cites evidence that happy marriages are by no means

1

on the wane. In the last 10 years a trend has emerged whereby couples are periodically reaffirming their marriage vows in the presence of friends and family. Often the renewal takes place in church and couples participate in a joint ceremony. It is a chance to say, 'My choice of partner was a good one, and I am willing to go on being responsible for that choice.'

Against this encouraging background we turn now to some official statistics for marriage and divorce. The table below shows figures compiled by various governments for the number of marriages and divorces in 1979.

Country	Marriages	Divorces
Australia	104,396	37,854
Belgium	65,476	13,499
Denmark	27,842	13,044
England and Wales	368,853	138,706
France	340,405	89,800
Jamaica	8,949	756
Japan	788,505	135,250
Netherlands	85,648	23,748
Sweden	37,300	20,322
USA	2,331,337	1,181,000

We should remember that 1,181,000 divorces in the USA that year involved 2,362,000 people and their children. The right-hand column represents a vast human problem. The next table translates the one above into a 'per 1,000 of population' format, the standard international means of measuring and comparing trends in this field.

Country	Marriages	Divorces
Australia	7.2	2.6
Belgium	6.6	1.37
Denmark	5.4	2.55
England and Wales	7.5	2.8
France	6.4	1.69
Jamaica	4.2	0.35
Japan	6.8	1.17
Netherlands	6.1	2.86
Sweden	4.5	2.45
USA	10.6	5.3

The figures for Jamaica and even Japan suggest a pretty stable picture whilst those for Sweden and the USA for instance, are worrying. In 1980 the US Department of Health and Human

Services published its annual *National Estimates of Marriage Dissolution and Survivorship.* Surveys carried out in 1976 and 1977 indicated that an American marriage, on the wedding day, has only a 53 per cent chance of survival. If it lasts five years, it has a 63 per cent chance, and so on as the marriage grows older. Ten-year marriages have a 75 per cent chance of lasting whilst only six per cent of marriages which reach 25 years go on to end in divorce.

Latest figures for the United Kingdom *(Population Trends Summer 1983)* show 145,000 divorces in 1981. Where the groom is a teenager the marriage has only two chances in five of succeeding. The proportion of teenage marriages that end in divorce is twice that for those who marry between the ages of 20 and 24.

The number of people getting divorced is greater than ever before. Then there are others, close to the parties, who are emotionally or socially involved in the results of the breakdown of the relationship. This, in part, accounts for changing attitudes to cohabitation—living as if husband and wife, but not having gone through a marriage ceremony. In Britain and elsewhere the proportion of people cohabiting rather than marrying is increasing and there are signs that public opinion does not altogether disapprove. Even the older generation is shifting its stance. A recent UK poll concluded that less than half of those aged 65 or over believe cohabiting to be morally wrong *(Families in the future: A policy agenda for the 80s,* Study Commission on the Family, 1983).

Some young people reject marriage in favour of cohabitation because they resent the social ostentation which the wedding day frequently occasions. Some parents take it as an opportunity to display the family's affluence or social standing. The day is treated as if it were the parents' not the couple's. Clearly this emphasis is misplaced. Dignified simplicity is the hallmark of a salvationist wedding, where ostentation is discouraged.

The drift toward cohabiting is one into which salvationists ought not to be drawn. The fashion of the day will bring its own pressures, but our young people need to be equipped with sound, strong doctrine to withstand that which is trendy but wrong. The youngster who asks, 'But why do we need a legal transaction or a "bit of paper"?' deserves a firm, considered, but gentle reply. First, he needs to think out for himself the basic, commonsense reasons for marriage. Then these can be reinforced by reference to God's revealed will in Scripture.

Suppose you were invited to turn back the clock of human history and to devise some sort of system for regulating human sexual impulses. Starting completely from scratch you would probably take first into account the fact that human sexual

3

relations can produce new human beings! You would then remember that inbreeding can undermine the health of the community and so you would wish to record which couples had children, and would then enact measures to ensure, as far as practicable, that sexual relations did not occur between couples within certain close kinship degrees. All of this would be made easier if you had some way of recording which couples were producing children. It would make sense to you to require those intending to embark on a reasonably long-term sexual liaison to have their intention publicly registered for the good ordering of society as a whole. In other words, you have devised a system closely resembling what we know as 'marriage'.

Of course, marriage is much more than a mere system. It is mutual loving, supporting, encouraging. It is self-giving, companionship and togetherness, come what may. It is lifelong commitment, a growing into 'one flesh'. It is, at its best, emotionally and psychologically conducive to wellbeing. But if we take it merely at the level of a social system, it still makes good sense.

There is, however, the specifically Christian dimension. Searching the Bible for a clear command, 'Thou shalt marry and not cohabit', will end in disappointment. But so too will a search for 'Thou needst not marry if thou preferest to cohabit'. However, there is help to be had. Genesis 2:24 speaks of a man and woman leaving their families to be joined in a 'one flesh' bond. This is an explicit reference to marriage in a passage which the publishers of the *New English Bible* have headed: 'The beginnings of history'. In other words, marriage, a public uniting of a man and a woman, is recorded in Scripture as an integral element in the story of creation. Richard Bewes, Rector of All Souls, Langham Place, London, puts it this way: 'Marriage actually goes back to the very beginning of things. Quite regardless of pieces of paper, it is a creation ordinance.'

The New Testament evidence is weighty. Jesus chose a wedding ceremony as the setting for his first public demonstration of divine power (John 2). He did not decline the invitation to the celebrations. He honoured the couple by his presence as he still honours those who invite him to preside on their special day. Later in John's gospel (chapter 4) we find him astonishing a woman he had met beside a well by telling her, scarcely with approval, that the man she was living with was not her husband. Then again, the honour deservedly accorded to marriage amongst Christians is conclusively affirmed by the startling comparison made in Ephesians 5. There the concept of marriage is used to illustrate and clarify the relationship between Christ and his body on earth, the

4

Church. It is a relationship for all the world to see. It is permanent and honourable. It is sealed by promises. Christ does not say to his Church, 'Let us see if we are compatible. I may want to abandon you if it suits me.' Instead he says, 'I have chosen you. I love you and I cherish you, for ever. Let all men know that this is how we stand with one another.' Do we need a clearer word from God on the rightful place of marriage amongst his children?

Thus it is that Christians choose marriage, not cohabitation. It is good sense for society. It is the way God wants it to be. A Christian wedding sees the couple making promises to each other in the presence of their Christian friends and relatives and in the presence of God who is expressly invited in prayer to preside over the ceremony. The Christian community openly witnesses the sacred transaction between the couple and, by its very presence, says to the newly weds, 'We love you, we will support and encourage you in your marriage, and we will be on hand to help when help is needed. We will pray for your happiness.' There is no better start to a lasting bond of love between a man and a woman.

Salvationists, in their personal living, have never been slow to stand apart from the fashions of the world in matters of morality. But that is not to say they wax judgmental toward those whose life-style would find no place in Army circles. The Army spends much time and energy working for the physical, spiritual and moral welfare of many a cohabitee. At the same time, where circumstances permit, the value and benefits of marriage are made clear and sometimes the Army is able to provide a marriage ceremony, invoking God's aid for the couple as they make new vows and regularise their relationship. Thereafter support is offered to the family as a whole. Often, the initial desire to marry after years of cohabiting is the direct result of a spiritual conversion to Jesus Christ. Sometimes marriage is ruled out if one partner is already married. In such cases, responsibilities assumed over years and commitments given, albeit informally, cannot be thrown over, especially where there are children of the liaison. Breaking off such a sexual relationship will be called for if the demands of purity are to be met. In most instances the many conflicting issues will be best unravelled with the aid of a skilled Christian counsellor whose task will be to balance principle with practicality.

Strong doctrine, but strong mercy is the order of the day.

2

Marriage and divorce (2)

MOST legal systems of the world provide for divorce. Recent years have seen marked changes in many countries with regard to the grounds on which a divorce may be obtained and also changes in procedure resulting in speedier divorces. The laws of England and Wales (overseas readers in other lands are asked to allow the reference, as the writer has no expertise in the laws outside England and Wales) have followed the widespread tendency to remove from divorce proceedings a determination of the guilt or innocence of the spouses. This chapter will trace these recent developments before examining the main New Testament statements on divorce.

The classic definition of marriage in English law was laid down in 1866: 'Marriage, as understood in Christendom, may . . . be defined as the voluntary union for life of one man and one woman to the exclusion of all others.' Every word in this definition is crucial. The parties to the marriage are said to have entered into a contract to marry, that contract being satisfied by the solemnisation of the marriage. There is thus created in law a specific relation between the parties. Mutual rights and duties arise and the parties have conferred upon them a new legal status, that of being 'a married person'.

If this then is marriage, the parties are said to be divorced upon the dissolution of the marriage bond and are deprived of 'married' status. The last 20 years or so have seen rapid change in the divorce laws of many lands. In England the Matrimonial Causes Acts 1950-65 were based on the idea of the 'matrimonial offence' and the giving of a remedy to an 'innocent' spouse against a 'guilty' spouse. P. M. Bromley *(Family Law)* expressed the view of many when he said, 'To insist that divorce should be available only if a matrimonial offence has been committed lays stress upon the symptoms of breakdown rather than on the breakdown itself.'

So 1966 saw two major statements on divorce law reform. The

6

first was *Putting Asunder,* a report by a group set up by the Archbishop of Canterbury. This concluded that the 'matrimonial offence' concept should be replaced by the 'breakdown of the marriage' as the sole ground for divorce. It advocated (as a safeguard) a judicial inquest in each case. The second statement was *Reform of the Ground of Divorce: the Field of Choice,* issued by the Law Commission. This saw as impracticable some of the suggestions of *Putting Asunder* but went on to say that the aim of a good divorce law should be 'to buttress, rather than undermine, the stability of marriage, and when, regrettably, a marriage has irretrievably broken down, to enable the empty legal shell to be destroyed with the maximum fairness and the minimum bitterness, distress and humiliation.'

This resulted in the passing of the Divorce Reform Act 1969 which took effect on 1 January 1971 and enacted that the sole ground for divorce would be 'that the marriage has irretrievably broken down'. This Act is now re-enacted in the Matrimonial Causes Act 1973 which forms the basis of English divorce legislation as it stands today. One vital provision of the 1973 Act is that attempts must be made at every stage in the proceedings to effect a reconciliation between the parties. The solicitor is duty bound to give his client details of where to obtain professional marriage guidance and the divorce proceedings can be adjourned at any stage if a reconciliation seems likely. Strict provisions are laid down which safeguard as far as possible the interests of any children affected by the divorce.

Christians, of course, will want to seek guidance on moral issues less from the law than from the pages of Scripture and so any Christian view of divorce must give an adequate account of the New Testament statements on the subject. But here we meet a major problem. Both Mark and Matthew report the same basic saying of Jesus on divorce but with sufficient variations one from the other to suggest that the writers of these gospels were to some degree confused as to what exactly Jesus had said. Let us look first at Mark 10:2-12.

Mark makes the conversation between Jesus and the Pharisees stem from the question: 'Is it lawful for a man to divorce his wife?' In view of Deuteronomy 24:1-4, which recognises plainly the legality of a bill of divorce, it seems that the Marcan form of the question is unlikely in an historical sense. The parallel question in Matthew 19:3 is given in a form historically more probable: 'Is it lawful to divorce one's wife for any cause?' Matthew therefore makes the topic of conversation the scope of a bill of divorce whereas Mark makes it the initial validity of any bill of divorce.

7

In Mark the Pharisees then go on to summarise the position under Mosaic law, saying that Moses allowed bills of divorce. The point of Jesus' reply is that Moses was making a concession to human weakness. Jesus says that their 'hardness of heart' (or refusal to obey God's will) had resulted in a frustration of the divine purpose summed up in Genesis 2:24: 'Therefore a man leaves his father and his mother and cleaves to his wife, and they become one flesh.' In other words, Genesis 1:27, which distinguishes male from female, has to be qualified by Genesis 2:24 which envisages the creation by marriage of a bond which, theologically speaking, is as indissoluble as the blood tie between a man and his parents.

Mark 10:10-12 has Jesus pronouncing that divorce is wrong whatever the reason. The underlying assumption seems to be that all divorce is a sin against God (in view of Genesis 2:24) and moreover that a subsequent remarriage would constitute adultery, thereby adding a second sin to the first.

We have already noted that the question put to Jesus in Matthew 19:3-9 differs from the one he answered in Mark. A second difference between the two accounts is that Matthew stresses the contrast between the word 'command' as used by the Pharisees in verse 7 and the word 'allowed' as used by Jesus in verse 8. That is, Jesus emphasises that Moses intended not a command but a permission or concession where God's ideal will had been frustrated by human weakness.

Perhaps the most striking (and most baffling) difference between the two gospel accounts occurs in verse 9. Mark 10:10-12 records a total prohibition by Jesus upon divorce but here in Matthew we are told that Jesus allowed an exception in the case of 'unchastity' (Greek: *porneia*). The scope of the exception is far from clear since *porneia* could mean either pre-marital fornication or post-marital adultery. Most commentators prefer the second meaning. But one thing at least is clear. The irreconcilable statements at Mark 10:10-12 and Matthew 19:9 make it impossible to 'read off' a divorce ethic from the synoptic gospels. If the Early Church found it difficult to discover the mind of Jesus on the issue of divorce, then how much more of a problem it is for us!

Nevertheless, the two passages discussed so far are not altogether empty of guidance. We can extract from them in general terms some idea of what Jesus thought. These gospel passages are not designed for use as a rulebook. We have to tease out not rules but principles. Thereafter, we are left to work out the rules for ourselves from the principles in reliance on the Holy Spirit and the accumulated wisdom of the Christian community. Two main principles are discernible here. It would appear that Jesus distinguished between two orders in the world and human affairs. The first order is that indicated by the words 'from the beginning' (Mark 10:6 and Matthew 19:8). This is the order of God's eternal purpose for man in which the rule is: 'no divorce'. Even Moses cannot alter this. The second order is that signified by the phrase 'for your hardness of heart' (Mark 10:5 and Matthew 19:8). This is the order of things as they now stand in an imperfect world infested with sin and for which the rule is: 'divorce within limits'. This second order is a concession to realism and it falls to the Church to work out for itself, just as Moses had to work them out in his day, what the proper limits must be when God's original intention is perceived to have been frustrated by man. Despite such frustration, the Church has to continue to witness to the eternal validity of the first order rule by retaining the 'for life' vows in the marriage ceremony. In other words, Christians, salvationists among them, stand as it were with one foot in Heaven and one foot very much on earth. We have to find some way of holding in tension not only the integrity and inviolability of marriage but also the need to cater compassionately for the vagaries of human nature. Again, it is a case of strong doctrine with strong mercy.

Some Christian bodies, for example the Church of England, have in the past interpreted the gospel statements on divorce in a way that prohibits the remarriage in church of any divorced person. On the other hand the free churches and The Salvation Army are prepared—in certain closely examined circumstances—to marry a divorced person. Each case is considered on its merits. No automatic bar to remarriage is felt to exist merely because of there having been a divorce. No doubt there divergent attitudes both spring from a desire to safeguard the institution of marriage. But the signs are that the rigid approach of the anglicans is changing to something more flexible. In July 1981 the General Synod of the Church of England asked its Standing Committee to prepare a document listing the range of procedures for cases where it might be thought appropriate for a divorced person to marry in church during the lifetime of a former partner (see now *Marriage—and the Standing Committee's Task,* CIO Publishing, 1983).

The Army issued a positional statement on marriage on 29 November 1982 which stressed that the movement has no option but to recognise 'the reality that some marriages fail' but that 'where remarriage could lead to the healing of emotional wounds, the Army will permit its officers to perform a marriage ceremony for a divorced person'. The statement continues: 'Sound doctrine, with practical mercy are the hallmarks of the salvationist's approach to marital and emotional strife.'

The Christian Church is commissioned to bring to wrecked and wounded lives the healing power of the gospel. Sometimes a divorce wrecks and wounds as nothing else does. When this happens the Church must be on hand to bring healing and renewal. In certain cases these may come about only in a second marriage.

Some Christians have felt genuine concern at the recent trends in the reform of the divorce laws of England. But the question which arises is whether Christians can reasonably expect the civil law to be a model of Christian ethics when Christians are now in a minority in society and in any case cannot agree amongst themselves what the law ought to be. We have to ask ourselves, as C. S. Lewis put it in *Christian Behaviour,* 'how far Christians, if they are voters or Members of Parliament, ought to try to force their views of marriage on the rest of the community'. Is it a Christian's duty to try to make divorce difficult for everyone? Is marriage best safeguarded by forcing couples to live together in an empty relationship from which love has long since vanished?

Perhaps we should begin our thinking on these questions by admitting frankly that most people today are not Christians and therefore cannot be expected to live Christian lives.

C. S. Lewis advocates the establishing of two distinct kinds of marriage. One would be for all citizens and organised by the State. The other would be for Christians only and supervised by the Church. At least this would allow us to recognise, says Lewis, which couples are married in a Christian sense and which are not. It is an idea worth exploring.

Meanwhile, Christian men and women must witness to the sacramental nature of marriage, marriage as a means of grace and healing.

> *Let us go deeper*
> *you and I*
> *for we belong together*
> *and love's image dwells within*
> *God's you and I;*
> *we must explore*
> *in prayer*
> *and find the real each other,*
> *awareness growing all the time*
> *for each is for the other*
> *in the likeness of Christ's mind.*

(*Exploration into Love,* quoted by J. W. Bowker in *Marriage, Divorce and the Church,* SPCK, 1971).

3

Artificial insemination and inovulation

THE pain of longing for a child and the gradual realisation that no child will be conceived is not one to be underestimated. In the United Kingdom, for instance, there are 1,000,000 infertile married couples and eight per cent of all marriages remain childless after 10 years. It is claimed that between one-third and one-half of all problems of this kind are due to male infertility. The pain caused to many through childlessness will arouse strong compassion, strong mercy in the heart of the salvationist.

Some couples adopt, some foster, a child. Others settle for a life without children of their own and constructively redirect their time and interests. Still others pursue by all available means their quest for parenthood and it is these who are most likely to be offered the fruits of the biological revolution.

The technique of artificial insemination (AI) has been with us for almost a century now. Its counterpart, artificial inovulation, is of more recent date, but is equally far reaching in its possibilities. We live now in an age when experimentation on human embryos is possible outside the womb, when embryos may be bought and sold, when embryos may be transplanted into the womb of any willing woman whether she produced the egg or not (surrogate motherhood), and when the practical possibility exists of selecting an embryo with particular characteristics, including the sex, prior to implantation. Artificial insemination, artificial inovulation and embryo transfer represent great advances in the treatment of infertility but there are some aspects of current practice which might cause concern to Christians. Before discussing the techniques, let us remind ourselves of the strong doctrine to which we subscribe concerning human life.

The ultimate source of all human life is God. Life is a gift of God

11

and all human life is sacred. Human beings are more than physical. We are a complex unity of body, mind and spirit, each of these acting upon and reacting with the others. We are accountable to God for what we make of his gift of life. He has pronounced (see Jeremiah 1:4, 5) that we are known by him individually even before we are conceived and that he loves us with an infinite love. There are factors in the mind of God, not necessarily known to man, which govern the working of the created world and the creation of new human lives. These factors have sometimes been described as 'divine randomness' and insofar as man intermeddles in the natural order he must ensure that he co-operates with God, overcoming the universal temptation to usurp him. Mankind has achieved precious insights flowing from the coming and teaching of Jesus and we would hold that the reproduction of human beings ought not to take place at the expense of these: the sanctity 'of marriage, the respect due to the dignity of human beings and their bodies, the need for openness and truthfulness about human relationships, the value of technology to assist or enhance (not replace) natural or instinctive capacities and, finally, the need to protect weak and vulnerable members of society, particularly the children, whether born or as yet unborn.

These beliefs about human life counsel extreme caution and the utmost accountability to the public on the part of those engaged in modern practice relating to human fertilisation and embryology.

Artificial insemination may involve the use of semen collected from the husband (AIH) or from a donor (AID). There appear to be few ethical problems related to AIH. For example, it would be entirely acceptable where the husband suffered from sex-related psychological problems or perhaps faced castration because of some malignancy.

The ethics of AID are more complicated. The first recorded case was in 1884 at the Jefferson Medical College in the USA, involving a couple where the husband was infertile. The identity of the donor was not revealed, but in a letter to the journal, *Medical World,* in 1909, it was claimed there had been a successful conception. The technique was not widely used or even known until the *British Medical Journal* carried a full account in 1945. Thereafter, a Commission appointed by the Archbishop of Canterbury reported in 1948, recommending that the practice of AID should be made a criminal offence. A government report in 1960 did not go quite so far, but concluded that AID was socially undesirable (Feversham Departmental Committee on Human Artificial Insemination). In the past 20 years, there has been a marked shift in opinion encouraged by the results (made public in 1973) of a British Medical Association inquiry under Sir John Peel.

The AID technique is medically straightforward. The donor deposits seminal fluid into a simple container. This is then delivered swiftly for immediate use or for freezing and storage. The procedures for freezing are complex, involving the use of a cryoprotective medium and liquid nitrogen. The thawing procedures are equally delicate. For the purpose of insemination, the recipient will keep an accurate record of her monthly body cycle and basal body temperature so that insemination may take place near the time of ovulation, the optimal time for conception.

Demand for AID is growing. A spokesman for the British Pregnancy Advisory Service, on the launching of a nationwide AID scheme, said: 'Our service will open up a whole new era. We are expecting thousands of inquiries from women who cannot conceive because of their husbands. We would not necessarily turn away an unmarried woman who wants to have a baby by AID and the same would apply to lesbian couples.' In 1973 the Peel Report estimated that one-third of all couples where the husband was infertile would consider using AID. It is worth adding that infertility is not the only motivation. A husband may suffer from a hereditary disease or he may have entered a second marriage following a vasectomy. At a public lecture in June 1982, the director of an AI clinic in the United Kingdom stated that his two partners had carried out at least 1,000 AID procedures each. In France there are 12 AID centres registered by the central government. No system of registration or control exists in the United Kingdom. This is to be regretted.

Before focusing on the ethical issues involved, a word on the legal aspects. In England and Wales an AID child is illegitimate although the practice of AID is not itself illegal. In registering the birth, entry of the husband's name as the father amounts to contravention of the Perjury Act 1911. In 1979 the Law Commission recommended that the mother's husband be deemed to be the legal father of an AID child (*Family Law: Illegitimacy,* Working Paper No 74). This would, or course, create anomalies in the case of an AID child born to a single or lesbian parent. In Switzerland AID is illegal. In the USA the position varies with the state. In California, Georgia and Oklahoma, AID is legal and AID children are seen as the legitimate offspring of the couple, provided that the husband consented in writing to the insemination. However, proposals to legalise AID have been rejected in Indiana, Minnesota, New York, Virginia and Wisconsin. The main difficulty resulting from legal systems not designed to cope with AID births is that of the falsifica-

13

tion of records. It is a deceit upon the child and upon society as a whole.

Serious doubts have been raised about the ethical acceptability of AID. The longing for parenthood is natural and, when unfulfilled, painful. But can we say that to fulfil that longing by *any* means is morally acceptable? There is scarcely any area of human life in which we grant an absolute, unconditional right to anyone to have a particular desire met. Becoming a parent is no exception. It may help to look at the issue from the point of view of each of the persons involved: *(a)* The couple; *(b)* The donor; *(c)* The child; *(d)* The medical practitioner.

(a) The pressures on the couple to have a child are socially as well as emotionally powerful. It is not hard to feel for the man who wrote to the Feversham Committee, 'I could not condemn my wife not to bear a child'. In such a case AID is seen as satisfying the wife's maternal instinct whilst at the same time successfully hiding the fact of the husband's sterility. It is arguable whether the stress of childlessness outweighs the stress of conceiving, bearing and rearing an AID child.

Professor G. R. Dunstan, recently retired from the F. D. Maurice Chair of Moral and Social Theology at King's College, University of London, has said: 'If the spouses believe there is a nexus between marriage and begetting so strong and exclusive that any invasion of it from without is wrong, even though extra-marital conception can be achieved without adulterous sexual union, they will not ask for AID.'

Of course, a husband cannot be condemned for wanting to please his wife, for wanting perhaps to save his marriage, for wanting a child at least 50 per cent 'theirs', for wanting to appear 'normal' to society or for wanting an heir. He has to find some means of coping with a sense of inadequacy. This sense can, however, only be intensified by the arrival of a child not his own. He may well have agreed to the insemination to make up to his wife for his (so called) failure. The child is proof positive that his wife and another man, not a party to the marriage, have succeeded where he has failed. In cases of adoption, the adopting parents share an identical relationship to the child and society knows of and approves of the husband as the social, not the genetic, father. In cases of AID, shrouded as they are in secrecy, the husband pretends to all but his wife and the medical practitioner that he is the genetic father. In fact, the donor is the father.

The wife's feelings are not less complex. She is able to bear a child and yet the man to whom she is deeply committed constitutes an impediment. Her expectation of motherhood and her expectation that her husband will be active in creating the child have both been denied. The first expectation can be satisfied only at the cost of the second. There will follow embarrassing interviews, examinations, procedures which she will resent for, after all, she is the 'normal' one. In all of this she will have to support her husband and somehow cushion his mounting sense of inadequacy. Many AID wives have reported intense feelings of guilt at their willing involvement of an outsider to the marriage. Some even refuse anaesthetics during confinement for fear of revealing involuntarily the secret of the child's origins.

Secrecy surrounds all aspects of AID procedures. Just how couples are selected or screened is not known. The need for secrecy discourages the seeking of independent assessments on suitability and so the selection is narrowly confined to the family doctor and the AI practitioner. This would seem too limited a procedure, made worse by an absence of clear criteria. No answer has been given in the United Kingdom to the questions: 'who selects?' 'who is selected?' and 'why?'.

(b) In all cases the donor remains anonymous, a shadowy figure not only behind but somehow between the couple. In France they call him 'the stranger'. No one knows how he is selected, save that often medical students are used and, frequently, paid for their services. It has been said that he is screened for intelligence, health and a general physical resemblance to the infertile husband. Total responsibility for selection falls here upon the AI practitioner since anonymity demands that he alone be involved in choosing the donor. This selection proceeds without any external regulation of any kind. The number of offspring from each donor is unknown. Successful donors are likely to be used many times over and thus the risk of half-brother and half-sister eventually mating is increased. Any harmful recessive genes in such a donor spread repeatedly into the population and it has been claimed that a single donor might father not tens but hundreds of offspring.

One might wonder what motivates a donor; whether he has doubts about the rightness of his involvement; whether he has any opportunity properly to assess the implications or whether his judgment is impeded by pressure (in the case of medical students) from staff and teachers or even by the offer of pecuniary reward. What sort of man voluntarily puts himself in a position so fraught with possibilities for embarrassment, especially where there is resort to furtive measures to keep donor and recipient apart in the event of the donated material being used immediately and unfrozen? The German Lutheran theologian, Helmut Thielicke, asks, 'What degree of human degeneration or what degree of

15

primitive under-development in instincts and ideas is required to play the role of an anonymous spermator?' It is no answer to liken his action to that of a donor of blood, for blood does not carry reproductive potential.

The donor, as the biological father, turns his back on the responsibilities normally associated with parenthood and procreation. Anonymity cannot cancel responsibility. Neither can the absence of sexual intercourse. How acceptable is it in the light of Christian thinking to 'parent' a child you do not want, for whom you intend from the start to abandon all responsibility, and whose mother is a total stranger to you? The Feversham Committee reported: 'We feel that the role of the donor is of such a kind that it is liable to appeal to the abnormal and unbalanced.'

Married donors are in an even less defensible position for obvious reasons. It is not known whether AI practitioners insist that a married donor must have the prior consent of his wife to the procedure but such insistence should be a minimal requirement. It is not an answer to assert that a man's body is his own. No one has an absolute right over himself. For instance, we limit the right to abortion and we regard suicide as morally dubious. There is a sense in which a man's procreative capacity belongs to the whole of society, more particularly to his wife, his existing children, even to a possible future spouse, for no man is an island, a law unto himself.

(c) Clearly, an AID child is planned and wanted. That is a good start, but other factors supervene which may render the child's security less sound. Almost all AID children are unaware of their origins, for voluntary informing of the child is very rare indeed. Of those who do learn the truth it must be assumed that they discover it by accident, perhaps when a marriage breaks down. Research on a proper basis is impossible since secrecy surrounds every case. We are ignorant of the long-term sociological and psychological effects of AID upon the children so conceived. What is clear, however, is the climate of deception in which the child is reared. AID becomes a family secret, the cause of sudden silences in conversation, warning glances behind the child's back. The legal status of the child is far from clear, but he has no right, in the United Kingdom, to have access to data on his biological origins, although recommendations have been made which would change the law to allow an AID child knowledge, not of the identity of the donor parent, but of the genetic details of that parent (see below on the Warnock Report).

(d) For the medical practitioner the ethics are made complex by diverse social attitudes and the inadequacy of the law. No official

16

approval has been forthcoming for the practice of AID in Britain. At the same time, it is not outlawed. The churches have expressed clear disapproval (see the report of a working party set up by the Free Church Federal Council and the British Council of Churches, *Choices in Childlessness,* March 1982). We still await the outcome of inquiries set up recently by the British Medical Association, the Royal College of Obstetricians and Gynaecologists and the Council for Science and Society. Present practice, in so far as it may be monitored, leaves cause for concern. We have seen that there is no common protocol for the selection of patients and donors or for the recording and publishing of data enabling objective assessment of results. At present, in the United Kingdom, the practitioner remains party to a legal offence (under the Registration Act 1965) and to a deceit upon society. Professor Dunstan lists the practitioner's duties thus: *(a)* to the spouses, a duty of diagnostic vigilance; *(b)* to the child, a duty of utmost care in the selection of the donor; *(c)* to the donor, a duty not to exploit or spoil him psychologically.

The use of AID will increase. Its misuse will therefore increase. Clear guidelines must be worked out for all concerned and the professions must regulate the practice closely and with care. Failing this, restrictive legislation will be needed around the world in those lands where clinics now function.

Many Christians will see the practice as unacceptable. It will be regarded as inimical to the marriage bond and as a real threat to the family as we know it. One leading writer in this field, Professor Robert Snowden of the Institute of Population Studies in the University of Exeter, has said: 'A woman will be able to have a child of her own without having to endure the gestation period, by a man who may or may not be her husband, or even known to her. Here, if ever, is the possibility of dispensing with the family as we know it today.'

The reference to the gestation period brings us to the counterpart of artificial insemination, artifical inovulation. This is the area of so-called 'test-tube babies' or *in vitro* fertilisation pioneered by Patrick Steptoe and Robert Edwards. (*In vitro* is Latin for 'in glass' and is in distinction to *in vivo,* 'inside a living being'.) It is now possible to fertilise a woman's egg with her husband's sperm outside her body. Then, at an early stage in the development of the embryo, it is inserted into the womb in the hope that this will lead to implantation and eventually a normal delivery. Some 100 children have now been born following *in vitro* fertilisation, and at the time of writing (mid-1983) the world's first test-tube baby, Louise Brown, has just celebrated her fifth birthday. No greater

17

risk is involved than with a natural conception. It is also possible to collect several ova (eggs) and fertilise them all, using one, whilst storing the remainder frozen for eventual use should implantation fail with the first. At a recent international gathering in Dublin Patrick Steptoe and Robert Edwards predicted that it might soon be more efficient than nature, producing more babies with fewer abnormalities. It is thought that 25 per cent of natural pregnancies go to full term as against 30 per cent of those resulting from *in vitro* fertilisation.

As with AIH, there appear to be no ethical complications with this method whilst it is limited to husband and wife. Steptoe and Edwards, the writer is informed, restrict the method to married couples. It is very different, however, once a third party is introduced. Many of the problems associated with AID apply equally to this situation. The donor now is the female who makes available her ovum for fertilisation *in vitro* with the intention that insertion of the embryo will be into the womb of another woman not the genetic mother of the child. This permits the carrying and delivery of a child by a woman regarded as infertile. Again, genetic and social parenthood are divorced.

We are at the stage where truly bizarre possibilities are opened up: surrogate motherhood; selection from sperm banks of 'super-dads' for 'super-babies'; conceiving one's son a century after one's death; the 'cloning' of infinite sets of identical twins. The foreseeable genetic permutations are now endless. What was science fiction 10 years ago is established practice now.

The dangers lie in confusing availability with acceptability. Available knowledge is usable knowledge. Since Hiroshima we know as never before that not all knowledge is good, but that all knowledge will be used. Christian men and women will arm themselves by forethought and foresight to avert a drift into biological anarchy. They will re-emphasise the truths inherent in God's staggering declaration to Jeremiah: 'Before I formed you in the womb I knew you for my own' (Jeremiah 1:5, *NEB*), reminding society that people are born for a purpose, that human lives are planned by God, that marriage is his gift and he wills its sanctity to remain intact. Similarly, that sex is his gift and steps to render it redundant fall outside his plan for the human race.

In some parts of the world the Army has been invited to offer opinion in these matters to governments as they formulate policy to regulate the new techniques. As part of this process, International Headquarters submitted written evidence, early in 1983, to the British Government to be used by the committee of inquiry chaired

18

by the Oxford moral philosopher, Dr Mary Warnock. The committee's terms of reference were as follows:

To consider recent and potential developments in medicine and science related to human fertilisation and embryology; to consider what policies and safeguards should be applied, including consideration of the social, ethical and legal implications of these developments and to make recommendations.

The Warnock Report was made public in July 1984, and attracted massive media attention. Reactions to it varied from 'Brilliant!' to 'Disastrous!' Among its main recommendations were:

1 The establishing of a new statutory licensing authority to regulate infertility research and services.
2 The availability of AID on an organised and supervised basis, with unlicensed services being a criminal offence.
3 The licensing of *in vitro* fertilisation services.
4 The licensing of research on human embryos, but not beyond the 14th day of growth.
5 Follow-up studies of children born as a result of the new techniques.
6 The maintenance of secrecy as to the identity of a donor of genetic material.
7 Counselling facilities at all stages of the procedures for all parties.
8 A limitation upon genetic donors so that no single donor could parent more than 10 children.
9 No payment of semen donors.
10 A maximum of 10 years for the frozen storage of embryos.
11 No placing of a human embryo in the uterus of another species for gestation.
12 No recruitment of women for surrogate pregnancy or making arrangements for surrogacy, on pain of criminal penalties.

Many Christians will be anxious that Warnock did not uphold marriage as the only proper context for human procreation, and possibly even more anxious that no protection is afforded human embryos under 14 days old. The two weeks limit is based upon the point at which the first signs of a central nervous system appear in the foetus. 'Thou shalt not kill' has been reduced to 'Thou shalt not cause pain'. It is also difficult to reconcile Warnock's vehement rejection of surrogate motherhood with its easy acceptance of surrogate fatherhood (AID).

The issues in this field of human assisted reproduction are many and complex. There are no very easy answers. Debate will and must continue and Christians must play their full part—that is, Christian doctors, theologians, lawyers, social workers, parents. It will be

19

difficult to balance strong doctrine and principle with strong mercy and sensitivity. For those seeking fulfilment in parenthood who are prepared to go to any length, the salvationist will not water down his beliefs, but neither will he utter one syllable of condemnation as he offers love and counsel in Christ's name.

4

Abortion

THIRTY-SEVEN thousand abortions were performed in Great Britain under the terms of the Abortion Act 1967 in the first year of its operation. By the end of 1983, according to government figures, 2,234,326 such abortions had been procured so that in Britain there is now one procured abortion to every five live births, or, to put it another way, a foetus is destroyed every four minutes. Even by 1973 the figure was in excess of 150,000 abortions annually, many apparently for no more than social reasons, and this prompted the publication in January of that year of an official Salvation Army statement on abortion.

This statement rightly urged 'that a Royal Commission or similar body be set up to study fully the social and ethical aspects of abortion, with a view to a basic revision of the 1967 Act'. It was also stated that 'the unborn child is a potential person from the moment of conception, and a potential member of a family and of society. . .'. This view is the cornerstone of the Army's stand against abortion on demand and therefore provides the best starting point for any discussion of the ethics.

The Army's view that the foetus must be regarded as a potential person from the moment of conception can be traced back at least as far as Tertullian, a brilliant North African theologian who lived from about AD 160 to about AD 220. He rejected the idea that the foetus should be seen merely as a growth on the mother's body and therefore removable at will. He said that the moments of quickening and birth played no role in the foetus becoming a person, for all the essential conditions of personhood were present as soon as conception took place.

Today the view of Tertullian on the status of the unborn child is the one we adopt, for the life of the newly-born baby differs not in kind but only in environment from the baby's life in the womb. A 1977 methodist statement, *Abortion Reconsidered* (Methodist

21

Publishing House), said: 'From the time of fertilisation, the foetus is a separate organism, biologically identifiable as belonging to the human race and containing all the genetic information. It will naturally develop into a new living human individual.' In 1974 a Papal Declaration on Procured Abortion stated: 'Respect for human life is called for from the time that the process of generation begins. From the time that the ovum is fertilised, a life is begun which is neither that of the father nor of the mother; it is rather the life of a new human being with his own growth. It would never be made human if it were not human already.' Modern knowledge of genetics supports this view. Implantation is the first stage following fertilisation in a continuous growth and development process. In the few days prior to implantation the zygote (the fertilised ovum or egg) becomes a grouping of mutually interchangeable cells containing all that it takes to become a person. Then the cells organise themselves to form various tissues and organs. After implantation (or nidation), when the cell mass attaches to the wall of the uterus, development over the next eight weeks or so sees the production of all the systems of the body. The foetus becomes viable—capable of surviving if born—at a point in the sixth or seventh month of the pregnancy, normally having 'quickened' or stirred in the womb during the fifth month.

The view that the unborn child is, if not a person, at least a potential person and certainly a human life is that presupposed by English Common Law which, when capital punishment was practised, forbade the hanging of a pregnant woman on the grounds that to hang her would be an assault upon the innocent life of her unborn child. Recent Common Law decisions have been welcomed which recognise the legal right of a child to sue for compensation for injuries received prior to birth. Many countries now accord such legal rights to the unborn child. In England, Wales and Northern Ireland the governing statute is the Congenital Disabilities (Civil Liability) Act 1976 which allows a child born disabled to sue for damages where the disability is caused by 'an occurrence which *(a)* affected either parent of the child in his or her ability to have a normal, healthy child; or *(b)* affected the mother during her pregnancy, or affected her or the child in the course of its birth, so that the child is born with disabilities which would not otherwise have been present'.

English law is in some confusion. The Abortion Act 1967 produces 2,000,000 dead foetuses in 16 years, whilst the Congenital Disabilities Act 1976 recognises the right of an injured foetus to sue after birth for compensation! Conclusion? It is cheaper to kill a foetus than merely to damage it! This cannot be logically or

22

morally acceptable. The position is further complicated since our Court of Appeal declared in February 1982 that a deformed foetus has no legal right not to be born and that a doctor is under no legal duty to terminate the life of such a foetus *(McKay v Essex Area Health Authority)*. The decision is a welcome one, but it throws into stark perspective the tension created by the 1967 Act between itself and other laws relating to the rights of the unborn child.

Readers outside the British Isles are asked to allow these references to the British legal scene, but they are not untypical of wider international developments reflecting the struggle by the pro- and anti-abortion lobbies to shape local legislation according to their respective views. In the USA in June 1983 the Supreme Court ruled by 6-3 votes that individual States may not place restrictions on a woman's right to have an abortion. Interestingly, the only woman member of the Court, Justice Sandra de O'Connor, wrote a dissenting judgment. Two weeks later the American anti-abortion movement suffered a second setback when the Senate rejected by 50-49 votes constitutional amendments which would have outlawed abortion. Sweden has had liberal abortion laws for years. Now a technique has been developed at Stockholm's Karolinska Hospital known as a 'do-it-yourself abortion kit'. The method allows women the option of terminating a pregnancy (otherwise known as killing an unborn child) at home, in private, without check or restraint. No wonder the manufacturers of the kit advise the taking of tranquillisers for a month prior to use!

In contrast, Belgium's laws are more conservative, but pressure is mounting for change. In November 1982 a press conference was called by 2,000 Belgian doctors to declare their intention to go on defying the law by carrying out illegal abortions. Many Roman catholic countries still do not permit abortion but France, after a bitter public debate in 1974, promulgated laws permitting abortions virtually on demand during early pregnancy. As the debate raged, the Vatican released a document condemning all legislation that would legalise abortion and in return was attacked for interfering in France's internal affairs. The issue invariably arouses feelings already intense. It should, since life itself is at stake and is precious. Now Spain is enduring what France endured a decade ago. There the issue of liberalising the law remains unresolved. In the Republic of Ireland, the end of 1983 saw a referendum of all voters on the abortion issue. Christian groups everywhere are urging the acceptance of a wider, not a narrower, definition of human life, in the interests of all human beings.

It is worth mentioning at this point a special issue in 1973 of the Roman catholic journal *Month*. The entire issue was devoted to the problem of abortion with contributions from experts in medicine, psychiatry, sociology, law and ecology. The opening article stated bluntly that Christians can best protect unborn children by broadening the grounds on which they argue against abortion. The writer went on to accuse many of his fellow catholics of 'rhetorical overkill', by which he meant that they had waxed eloquent in presenting religious arguments against abortion when addressing largely non-theists, ie, persons with whom an argument based on a belief in God would cut no ice at all. The article saw the status of the foetus as the central issue in the abortion debate and reiterated the view that the unborn child should be seen as alive, as an individual, and as a person in its own right. All of this lends strong and welcome support to the Army's view.

If the status of the foetus is that of a person in its own right, what may rightly be said to be the value of the foetus? Should we place on it an absolute value, that is, should we preserve it at all costs? It would seem not, for we do not place such a value on human life in general. We admit that there are exceptions to the rule that human life should never in any circumstances be forfeited, as for instance in the case of a self-defence response to an attack which threatens our own life. But we have to give the foetus an extremely high value, as high as that given to human life in general, so that the burden of proving the morality of ending the life of a foetus in any given case falls squarely on the one claiming the exception to the general rule of the sanctity of life.

This brings us to the question of individual cases. In what sort of circumstances should an abortion be seen as morally permissible? The Army's view is that 'abortion should continue to be legalised on adequate medical grounds, both physical and psychological, but not for social reasons'. So a pregnancy may reasonably be terminated when the physical or mental health of the mother is *seriously* threatened. The Abortion Act 1967 provides for this but goes much further, further than salvationists would wish. It permits an abortion if the pregnancy involves risk to the health of other children of the mother whether or not her own health is threatened. It is not easy to envisage occasions when an abortion would be justified on this ground.

The Act also allows a termination when there is a substantial risk that if the child were born it would suffer from such physical or mental abnormalities as to be seriously handicapped. The wise man would be very slow to pronounce upon the morality of aborting in a case of such abnormality, but it could be said that this provision in the Act ignores the sophistication of a modern community which should be equipped to care adequately for handicapped persons. It leaves out of account also the love and devotion which such persons may both give and inspire. Today medical science can, by means of a foetoscopy or amniocentesis, diagnose defects in the foetus well in advance of the birth. To assume automatically that abortion is always morally justified where a defect is found is to overlook that the quality of human life is much more than physical perfection.

It is understandable that many people tend to take the view that it is better to kill a severely handicapped foetus, this being in the interests of the family of which it would otherwise become a member. It is argued that the family's way of life would be unduly disrupted if the handicapped child were permitted to be born. Whilst easy to sympathise with this, it is an attitude which can lead to extreme results if the foetus is regarded as having all the constituents of human life. If we think that in most cases it is the best thing to kill a badly handicapped unborn child because the handicap threatens the domestic routine of the family then, if we are to avoid being logically inconsistent, we must also think that in most cases it is the best thing to kill other severely handicapped human beings. For example, it may be a child or even an adult who at any time encounters some disability which disrupts the family's routine. Few of us would be ready to go this far. We would be held back by all kinds of considerations, perhaps most of all by what Albert Schweitzer called 'reverence for life'. But if foetal life is human (or merely potentially human), why offer it less 'reverence', less protection, just because it is not physically perfect? In *The Clowns of God* (Hodder and Stoughton, 1981) Morris West imagines the return of the Lord to a crisis-stricken world. The Lord places on his knee a small girl with Down's Syndrome (Mongolism) and then addresses a small group of onlookers about his own divine identity: 'I know what you are thinking. You need a sign. What better one could I give than to make this little one whole and new? I could do it; but I will not. I am the Lord, not a conjuror. *I give this mite a gift I denied to all of you—eternal innocence.* To you she looks imperfect—but to me she is flawless, like a bud that dies unopened or the fledgling that falls from the nest to be devoured by the ants. She will never offend me, as all of you have done. She will never pervert or destroy the work of my Father's hands. *She is necessary to you.* She will evoke the kindness that will keep you human. Her infirmity will prompt you to gratitude for your own good fortune. More! She will remind you every day that I am who I am, that my ways are not yours, and that the smallest dust mote whirled in darkest space does not fall out of my hand. I have chosen you. You have not chosen me. This little one is my sign to you. Treasure her!' The italics are mine. The passage speaks for itself.

Many would argue in favour of abortion in cases where the child is conceived in unethical circumstances such as rape or incest or even where the mother is below the age of consent. Dogmatism on these suggestions is out of place. Perhaps the best approach here is 'every case on its facts', always remembering that society's interests are best served if we restrict abortion to narrower rather than broader limits.

Widespread abortion must eventually have a dehumanising effect on any society that encourages it. Non-Christians with permissive views on abortion have sometimes claimed that the desire to restrict the practice goes hand in hand with 'Christian narrow-mindedness' on sexual matters in general. There is evidence, however, that it is natural to the human species to restrict abortion fairly narrowly and that aversion to the artificial termination of pregnancies is not limited to Christian countries. Deep concern about the morality of some abortions cannot be dismissed as the result of what some non-Christians would call 2,000 years of Christian obscurantism since such concern is found even among the non-Christian Japanese. A survey carried out in 1972 shows that 59 per cent of Japanese non-Christian women thought abortion 'very wrong' whereas only eight per cent found 'nothing wrong' with it. Of women who had aborted (over 1,000,000 a year) 82 per cent said that they experienced feelings of guilt afterwards.

Finally, research has also been conducted into the relation between abortion and subsequent psychological disorder in the woman concerned. In a society which pretends that abortion is a trivial matter or merely a minor operation to be undergone as a means of easing the social inconvenience of a pregnancy, the women are being asked to live out a contradiction. On the one hand they are expected to assert life (by sometimes bearing children), but on the other they are expected to suppress life (by sometimes aborting). Living a contradiction results in conflicts and psychological disorder. In February 1973, the *Sunday Times* reported a Californian study which found that in the short-term the effect of an abortion was simply relief that the problem of the pregnancy had apparently been solved. But in the longer term the story changed dramatically, for within a few months over half the women in the survey were in need of psychiatric help. The pattern was one of 'acute depression, an inability to work, clinging to and immature dependence on parents, and in some cases promiscuity where before there had been steadiness'.

5

Voluntary euthanasia

IT has been said many times that death as a topic of conversation is taboo nowadays. There is, however, a healthy and vigorous debate going on about euthanasia. The word euthanasia means literally 'a good death' or 'gentle easy death', but at the present time it has come to mean the deliberate killing of someone who is suffering from a distressing and irremediable disease. That is the sense in which the term will be used in this chapter, which will confine itself to a consideration of voluntary euthanasia. So in this discussion we are concerned with direct killing and not with those cases where decisions are made to refrain from preserving life unreasonably by artificial means. Neither are we at the moment dealing with cases where drugs are given to relieve pain but which might also shorten the patient's life to some small degree. That is altogether another area of debate.

Euthanasia is said to be voluntary when the patient consents to being killed in order to escape the suffering his incurable disease may bring. It is the deliberate, requested extinction of a human life. Voluntary euthanasia stands over against the compulsory sort, when death is deliberately accelerated regardless of the wishes of the patient.

Early in 1983 the British press gave prominence to the deaths of Arthur Koestler and his wife. Koestler had been ill and was aged 77. His wife was not ill and was aged 55. They killed themselves in a suicide pact. Arthur Koestler came to prominence as an ardent advocate of voluntary euthanasia. He was vice-president of the British Voluntary Euthanasia Society and had published *A Guide to Self Deliverance* in the preface of which he said, 'The whole concept of death as a condition would be more acceptable if dying would be less horrendous and squalid. Thus euthanasia is . . . a means of reconciling men with their destiny.' This first sentence is right; the second is wrong.

27

Koestler's error was in identifying physical death as the 'destiny' of man. He left God out of account and therefore missed the truth that those who die in Jesus also come alive in Jesus who called himself 'Way, Truth and *Life*'. Man's rightful destiny is life with God. This is a fact needing not so much 'reconciliation' as joyful embracing.

Arthur Koestler's ideas have been influential upon many. One such is Gillian Tindall who commented in *The Times* (London) following the news of his suicide: 'So what about Koestler's suggestion of legalised "midwives" for death as for birth? It is an attractive and humane idea. . . . I am willing to bet that, within my own lifetime, ordinary people will look back with disapproval on the days when there were no proper arrangements for a timely death. . . . Like it or not, *it is coming*.'

The italics are mine, to emphasise the strength and persistence of the challenge to those, like the Army, opposed to euthanasia. Simplistic, misleading arguments abound in this field, such as: 'They do it for dogs; why not for humans?' The answer is that humans are not dogs and the considerations which might apply to ending the life of an animal are far less complex or morally charged than those which govern the premature ending of a human life. It may help to look at the legal position and then move on to the ethical arguments, both theistic and non-theistic.

In most countries of the world the legal position with regard to euthanasia is plain. Whether voluntary or otherwise, it means killing. A doctor is no different from an ordinary subject of the realm as regards his right to kill a dying patient. Professor Glanville Williams, an expert on English criminal law, writes: 'Under the present law, voluntary euthanasia would, except in certain narrow circumstances, be regarded as suicide in the patient who consents, and murder in the doctor who administers; even on a lenient view, most lawyers would say it could not be less than manslaughter in the doctor, the punishment for which, according to the jurisdiction and the degree of manslaughter, can be anything up to imprisonment for life' *(Sanctity of Life)*. If a doctor gives, for example, a fatal injection, he is almost certainly guilty of murder and it would be no defence that the victim gave his consent, or that he was suffering severe pain, or that he would soon have died in any case.

In January 1971 the British Medical Association (BMA) published a report entitled *The Problem of Euthanasia*. This comes out strongly against euthanasia of any description. It tries to put the matter into a proper perspective by stressing at the outset that 'some of the emotion behind the demand for euthanasia lies in the belief that death will be peaceful and dignified only after a lethal injection'. The report, which represents the official view of the British medical profession, emphasises that the vast majority of deaths are peaceful, whatever the preceding illness, and that, contrary to popularly held opinion, even the majority of patients suffering from cancer die peacefully.

What kind of case is usually put forward for legalising voluntary euthanasia? The literature of the Voluntary Euthanasia Society in Britain offers two main arguments. Firstly, it is urged that incurable patients are occupying scarce hospital resources which should be used for patients who have a chance of recovery. This is true. But why is the killing of incurable patients seen as the answer? In the circumstances, our moral duty is to increase the facilities available. Euthanasia is the easy answer. Like most easy answers it is the wrong one. After all, if you were running, say a bus service and found you were short of buses for the volume of passengers on your route, would you provide extra buses or would you put those waiting at the bus stops out of their misery by shooting them? The answer is self-evident, yet many refuse to see it when it comes to medical facilities and services for the dying. Perhaps more spent on hospitals and hospices and less on nuclear stockpiling . . . ? It would take a political decision on the allocation of national fiscal resources, but such decisions have been won before so that immediate human need is ranked before political posturing.

Secondly, it is argued that to kill a suffering and incurable patient if he requests it is the compassionate and merciful thing to do. Many are swayed by this argument. The use of words like compassion and mercy make it superficially attractive. Salvationists could never despise a suffering patient who, in desperation but in error, wished to die. Nor could they accuse of inhumanity a loved one who yielded mistakenly to the temptation to bring death artificially to a relative incurably diseased. The reasoning of the advocates of euthanasia can sway a person thus distressed. But careful thought will show where this kind of reasoning leads. If it is compassionate to kill a patient who is capable of consenting to euthanasia, it is logical to suppose that it is even more compassionate to kill one who by reason of his extreme condition is unable to consent. So we end up practising not voluntary, but compulsory, euthanasia. We thus find ourselves on a slippery slope to all kinds of horrors. Once we convince ourselves that it can sometimes be morally right to kill a man (in peace-time) against his wishes, we have begun to reverse the process of moral enlightenment which the centuries have unfolded. Moreover, such a view is incompatible with what the gospels teach about the value and sanctity of each individual human life.

29

Let us look now at the positive case against euthanasia. Some of the arguments against it are religious in nature and therefore appeal only to those with a belief in God. These are known as 'theistic' arguments. We shall outline first the 'non-theistic' arguments, those which do not depend for their validity on any religious belief.

Firstly, there is the familiar 'wedge' argument. This has been touched upon already in discussing the logical implications of the pro-euthanasia case. There is considerable force in saying that voluntary euthanasia, once legalised, would be the thin end of the wedge which could open the door for even more questionable practices. We live in an age when long-standing moral standards are gradually being eroded. If the law gives its blessing to voluntary euthanasia it would simply hasten that process of erosion. Moreover, Christians recognise that man is sinful by nature and any weakening of respect for human life will eventually be exploited and abused.

A second argument highlights the risk of diagnostic or prognostic error on the part of the doctors. The medical profession is respected for its high standards of skill but there is still a real possibility of a wrong diagnosis or simply some confusion in the patient's records. Mistakes here, as with capital punishment, cannot be put right. Let the BMA report speak for itself: 'Medical diagnosis, even though carefully made and supported by many tests, will always contain an element of fallibility. A recommendation for euthanasia would have to be based upon a diagnosis of irreversible physical or mental illness. Mistakes would inevitably be made.'

Thirdly, the whole concept of voluntary euthanasia is beset with difficulties relating to the nature of the consent given by the patient. This consent must be voluntary. To be valid it must be made by a person of sound mind. Yet an expressed desire for death may be a sign of a mental illness, in which case the request for euthanasia would be rendered invalid. If consent is given prior to the onset of the fatal disease, it has to be consent in view of some imagined future disease. This raises the question of whether a man can ever truly consent to being killed on the basis of what he may or may not be able to tolerate at some future date. If, on the other hand, consent is given at the time the disease is actually being endured, there are still problems.

In March 1969 an ultimately unsuccessful Voluntary Euthanasia Bill was introduced into the British House of Lords. This stated that the patient must be of a 'responsible' mind at the moment of consent. Yet it also required him to be suffering from some fatal disease expected to cause him severe distress or render him incapable of rational existence. Can consent be real in such circumstances? It is hard to envisage how a responsible state of mind and intolerable suffering can co-exist. If they cannot co-exist, voluntary euthanasia is a nonsense, a contradiction in terms. It has often been suggested that a card be devised which would be carried on the person like a kidney-donor card, but which would state the carrier's wish to be killed if, after the age of 65, some acute illness were to develop. Such a proposal was laid before the British Medical Association in June 1983 by Dr George Robertson, a consultant anaesthetist at the Aberdeen Royal Infirmary in Scotland. The BMA rejected the idea very firmly on the grounds that such a card would be irrelevant and unnecessary *since it is possible for patients to die in a confident frame of mind, pain-free and well-counselled.* The italicised words are medically and scientifically accurate and bring us to the fourth and perhaps most important reason for rejecting euthanasia.

The point is that there is a sound and proven alternative to the killing of dying patients, namely, good pre-terminal care and the skilled use of analgesic drugs. Writing in *The Times* (November 1974) about euthanasia Professor T. Symington, Director of the Institute of Cancer Research, states: 'Much can be done to relieve the physical, emotional and social distress that is encountered. Contrary to popular belief, the severe pain that all too often dominates extensive malignant disease can be alleviated, frequently abolished . . . the advocacy of euthanasia in such circumstances is increasingly irrelevant.'

In the same copy of *The Times* Dr R. G. Twycross, Research Fellow at St Christopher's Hospice, London, writes: 'It is important to appreciate that it is theoretically possible to relieve the pain in every case. . . . The account of a person dying in agony after weeks or months of unrelieved pain should increasingly become a thing of the past.'

The effective relief of pain is achievable in the vast majority of cases as the following figures show (from Appendix I of *On Dying Well*, Church Information Office, London, 1975):

1 Terminal patients admitted in one year to a hospice for the
  dying   577
2 Patients with no pain problem   228
3 Patients with pain problems   349
4 Patients with pain problems who obtained good relief   342
5 Patients remaining in pain   7

Of these seven patients whose pain problems were not relieved, only one wished to die and in her case there were psychological complications. Three out of the seven were in the hospice for less than two weeks. All seven received relief when sedated to the point of drowsiness. None of them had pain which was impossible to suppress under all circumstances.

Even Lord Raglan, the promoter of the 1969 Voluntary Euthanasia Bill, has admitted that the skilled and careful use of analgesic drugs in the care of the dying is a compelling argument against euthanasia. Agreeing with this view, the BMA has pointed out the need for more instruction in such matters to be given to doctors during their medical training. The need is for a change of emphasis and in attitudes rather than a change in the law.

Finally, but briefly, there is the whole question of the effect legalised euthanasia might have on doctor-patient relationships. Each consultation might arouse mistrust in the patient's mind. As Dr Duncan Vere says: 'The role of healer would be clouded by the role of death-bringer' *(Voluntary Euthanasia)*.

We now turn to some considerations which should weigh heavily with Christians. If God is the source of human life, the reasons for ending it must be more compelling than human consent or convenience. If seen as suicide, voluntary euthanasia might be rebellion against God and a denial of his providence. It presupposes that there is such a thing as a totally useless state of human life. It is born of hopelessness and despair, both of which are contrary to the spirit of the gospel. Any sentient state can still bear hope. The Christian sees the weakening of this physical life as a step toward a new life with God. Except in cases of accidental or sudden death, we think of the experience of contemplating the approach of death as a desirable, even necessary preparation for the life that is to come.

For the Christian, death points to man's utter helplessness before God and his ultimate dependence upon him. Faith requires us to wait upon God in patience. A request for euthanasia is no less than a refusal to trust a loving God. P. R. Baelz has called it 'an embracing of death for its own sake, a form of self-justification, a desertion to the enemy'. It is to abandon a waiting in hope in favour of a final act of despair.

6

Disobedience to the state

IS law sacrosanct? What is the Christian's duty to the state? These questions are difficult and this chapter cannot pretend to hold all the answers. Its aim is to summarise the thinking of noted Christians and to add a little comment along the way.

In 1975 the Army published a booklet called *Don't Sign Unless,* intended as a guide to those about to sign the articles of war thereby becoming soldiers of the Army. The booklet contained this statement: 'We pledge ourselves to disregard unrighteous law, just where we are.' Unexplained, this could well have revolutionary implications, but let us note an earlier passage: 'The Army condemns the use of violence in any part of the world. . . . We view with alarm the apparently ever-increasing deeds of violence, lawlessness, and disregard for human life and dignity.' It seems therefore that our stand is this—there is no duty to obey the law in all circumstances but, if we have to disobey, we shall not adopt violent means.

We are obliged to confine our utterances to statements of general principle and to leave it to those on the spot to decide how best to work things out in practice—a very practical matter if you live in certain parts of, say, Latin America or Southern Africa or communist Europe. When I was first preparing this material (it was in 1978 for an article in *The Officer* magazine) salvationists Diane Thompson and Sharon Swindells were shot dead at the Usher Institute in Rhodesia (now Zimbabwe). They were our friends and were buried in Bulawayo where we lived and worked. They were innocent victims in what has been called a 'liberation struggle'. Their fate is conclusive proof that even the best ideals degenerate in the hands of sinful men into a thirst for blood and a lust for power. Let us admit at once that it is hard to be objective in what we are about to discuss and perhaps that is why it is best to let voices from the history of Christian thought do the speaking.

First, however, we turn to the Scriptures. The reader should re-acquaint himself with Romans 13:1-7; 1 Corinthians 6:1-6; 1 Peter 2:13-17; Acts 5:29; Matthew 22:21 and even the obscurities of Revelation 13. Obviously, we cannot read off a clear-cut, absolute ethic from these combined passages. They were addressed to different audiences, written at different times and motivated by different situations. It is not fruitful to draw dubious parallels between present-day events and scriptural texts. Rather, seek the original meaning of the passage with reference to what was happening at the time it was written. Neither ought we to focus our attention exclusively on one particular passage, but try to balance each text with others of similar import. Most of all, our interpretation of a verse must be consistent with the overall thrust of the whole Bible, which is the message that God loves and cares for men and wants them, by his grace, to love and care for one another. Now let us turn to the theologians.

Thomas Aquinas (1225-1274) enjoys the distinction of having had his works proclaimed, by Pope Leo XIII in 1879, as the official Roman catholic philosophy. In his main treatise, *Summa Theologica,* he raises the question of a Christian's obligations to the state. He says that there is a duty to obey any power that comes from God and even to obey a ruler who proves personally to be unworthy to rule, since the office is greater than the one who fills it. But the duty of obedience is not absolute. A subject need not obey a ruler who has taken office by underhand means or by violence. Going still further, there is a positive duty to disobey (but only by passive means) a leader who acts contrary to the purpose and authority of his office. If the leader's misconduct does not clash with the purpose of his office but is nevertheless *ultra vires* (beyond his powers), then the subject has a discretion whether to obey or not. The teaching of Aquinas has much in common with the broad statement of the Army view outlined above. We can sometimes disobey, on occasion are bound to disobey, but never by more than passive, non-violent means.

Martin Luther's works are far removed from those of Thomas Aquinas both in date and content. Luther, greatest and most controversial of all the reformers, found himself obliged by force of circumstance to publish his views on revolution after the outbreak of the 1524 Peasants' Revolt in Germany. The revolutionaries found fuel for their ideals in Luther's theological writings, converting his 'priesthood of all believers' into a slogan of social equality and taking his 'freedom of the Christian man' not in its intended spiritual sense but as motivation for throwing off the bondage of feudal overlords. At first Luther remained silent on the civil disturbances, but within a year ransacking and pillaging had turned to violence and bloodshed. When he heard that he was being quoted in support of this he put pen to paper in *Warning Towards Peace*. He postulated two separate kingdoms, the spiritual and the secular. Both of these are God given. There is incumbent upon us a duty to obey the civil and secular authority even if this brings hardship. The state has been designed by God to curb evil so that the Kingdom of God might flourish and in this context revolution is one of the evils the state must curb. Rebellion against the government, writes Luther, is rebellion against God, and anyone resorting to force for social reform is no Christian.

Even while this was on the printing press, the violence escalated still further. Luther became convinced that the revolt was the work of the devil. Rashly, he published yet again with *Against the Murderous and Plundering Bands amongst the Peasants*. Described by one historian as 'biting, bitter vituperation' and as 'written in the heat of anger', it urged the authorities to 'smite, stab, slay' the offenders for 'there is nothing more devilish than a rebel'. They had broken their oath to the government, had robbed and murdered. Worst of all, they had done it in the name of the Christian faith thus committing blasphemy and disgracing God's holy name. The rebel, he wrote, was a 'mad dog' and thus had to be destroyed. Anyone who died in crushing the revolt had died, said Luther, a martyr's death. All this he based upon Romans 13.

In 1525 the authorities slaughtered 5,000 peasants at Frankenhausen just as Luther's second treatise came off the press. What he had written gave the bloodbath respectability. He could not win. Rome accused him of being the instigator of the rebellion, and the peasants saw him as a traitor to their cause. He was to write countless letters before it was all over, pleading for clemency for the rebels. He saw their fate as the judgment of God upon them, but at no time did he condone the action of the secular authorities, whose harsh treatment of the lower classes had sparked off the whole affair. To quote Luther in support of an absolute duty of obedience to the state is inviting disagreement, for his views were formed in the white-hot cauldron of the rebellion and in sharp reaction to events as they happened. Had he been able to offer us a more leisurely, detached analysis of a subject's duties to the state, we might have had a different story.

John Calvin wrote his *Institutes of the Christian Religion* in relatively calm conditions. Book IV claims that a civil ruler is God's 'ambassador' who enjoys 'a delegated jurisdiction from God'. Resisting him is resisting God. All this, of course, envisages a beneficent ruler. If the one in power is a tyrant, the private citizen still has a duty to obey him because even a bad ruler derives power from God. 'It belongs not to us to cure evils. All that remains to us is to implore the name and help of the Lord.' This may sound unduly helpless, but note that it relates only to the private citizen.

Where a state has some constitutional device for restricting an unworthy ruler, Calvin sees it as a positive duty to curb any abuse of power. But he stresses that this falls to the appropriate authority and not to the private citizen (eg, impeachment, not assassination). Failure so to curb a tyrant amounts to sin. If he demands obedience in a matter clashing with the commands of God, even the private individual may disobey, but by passive means only, and never to the extent of seeking to remove the ruler from office. That is not the role of the private man.

Dietrich Bonhoeffer brings us into the 20th century. Like Luther before him, his views were worked out upon the anvil of real events and in the end involved him directly in a plot to kill Hitler. The plot failed. Eventually to die for his view, Bonhoeffer saw the gospel of Jesus Christ as not merely for persons but for institutions too. Thus he felt called by God to work for the betterment and Christianisation of the state, of science, the economic structure, the educational system, etc. He saw all things existing in Christ: 'There is nothing that does not stand in some relation to Christ. Because of this all things are subject to Christ's word and claim.'

Bonhoeffer advocated a Christocentric theory of government. Government has its being in Christ. Its purpose is to serve Christ, and the cross of Jesus reconciles not only the individual and God but the institution of government and God. Hence there arises a duty to change what is inconsistent with Christ's claims. Failure to discharge that duty is a tacit admission that the world is not subject to the gospel. The Christian must obey the state, but not if obedience means offending his Lord. A government which expects a believer to act contrary to the gospel forfeits the right to govern. If the believer is in doubt in any particular case, then there is a duty to obey.

The views of these four great Christians should help us at least to sort out the issues at stake. Remember, too, that the state has no message of faith, of hope, or of love because only the gospel brings this to men. No Christian group can offer unreserved and absolute loyalty to the state, or even to a particular policy of the state, for policies are made and carried out by mortal and fallible men. Happily, the Army finds itself able, in normal circumstances, to co-operate with and to receive co-operation from governments around the world. But not all circumstances are normal and devout Christians have openly opposed, even offended, the secular authorities on occasion. Not invariably has the temptation to resort to violence been resisted. Some mention is made in the next chapter of 'liberation theology' which has attempted to justify the use of violence by Christians to change oppressive social systems. In *Christians, Politics and Violent Revolution* (SCM Press, 1976) J. G. Davies, Professor of Theology in the University of Birmingham, makes plain his sympathy with liberation theology. He sees the Christian gospel as seeking not to explain the world but rather to change it: 'Christianity is concerned to transform existence; it asserts the possibility of revolutionary change. This understanding of the gospel does not rest upon a few isolated texts; the good news is itself revolutionary.' Professor Davies then discusses a number of scriptural passages (John 8:32; Galatians 5:1, 13; Romans 8:21; Luke 4:18 f) and finds in them a Christian justification for revolutionary action leading directly to the overthrow of social structures and of governments. Not all biblical scholars would draw the same inference, however, and many might see these verses as applying primarily to the revolution which overtakes the individual heart of a man when he submits in faith to Jesus as Lord.

Professor Davies, though seeing in the New Testament a clear stimulus to social and political revolution, counsels great caution. The gospel 'should not be taken as a clarion call to Christians to rush hither and thither in a hot-headed attempt to start revolutions all over the place!' Dove-like innocence and serpent-like wisdom are needed. He writes: 'Revolution should not be regarded as a normal remedy, as a beneficial panacea, but as a last desperate operation. It carries with it certain serious risks.' The last sentence is an understatement. More than one freedom-fighter of today has become tomorrow's authoritarian dictator. Salvationists would point to the certainty of a revolution's failure where the revolutionaries are unwashed in the blood of Jesus but liberally stained in the blood of those they have overthrown. Even where violence appears to be the only option left, it is never the only option. But it is often a great seducer of those who set out to work for the poor or oppressed with high-minded and lofty ideals. Violence is never a solution, whether at the instance of the state or of revolutionaries.

At the heart of the gospel is the command to love as Jesus has loved us. His love for men and women did not and does not inflict, but absorbs, violence. Violence violates his command. It begins as a tool, but inevitably becomes an end in itself.

7

Race relations

AS an Army of the 'God of every nation', we have always taken pride in our internationalism. Bramwell Booth's declaration in 1912 is still true: 'The Salvation Army belongs to the whole world. It knows no nationality as such.' We can boast that the word 'foreigner' is not in our vocabulary, and this in an age beset by problems of race relations.

Which country has a history free from tribal or racial conflict? World Council of Churches documents define racialism as 'ethnocentric pride in one's own racial group and a preference for the characteristics of that group, believing these characteristics to be biological and hence transmitted to succeeding generations'. An alternative definition might be: 'The theory that some race or races are inherently superior to others and the organising of a society or a political economy on that basis.' The second definition is more realistic in that it indicates the effect racialism has on the allocation of votes ('political'), jobs ('economy'), on intermarriage and population distribution ('society').

It would seem important to admit, early in this chapter, that Christians carry their share of guilt for failing to be faithful examples of Christlike love to people of all races. The Army, reaching out to the needy and unconverted in some 85 countries, knows all too well the difficulties which can beset endeavours to preach the gospel in a racially charged atmosphere. These difficulties are not limited to where skin colours differ, but emerge even where colour is the same but tribes or nationalities and therefore languages differ.

In 1973, Joseph A. Ryan was the only white director of World Vision International. In *Christianity Today* (April 1973 issue) he wrote about communication problems between black and white Christians, saying, 'Three words seem to describe the white believer's attitude toward his black counterpart: isolation, ignorance, indifference. Ignorance and indifference are the brick and mortar that build the walls of isolation.' Ryan had in mind Christian communities in the USA when he penned these words, but they apply with equal force in many other lands.

Yet all is not lost. Even in those parts of the world regarded as a by-word for racialist practices, there are small signs of hope. The powerful, personal witness of many individual Christians there to the possibility of Christlike and mutual love and respect between all racial groups has received encouragement from a 1982 declaration by one sector of the Church in South Africa: 'We declare that apartheid (separate development) is a sin, that a moral and theological justification of it is a mockery of the gospel, and that its persistent disobedience to the word of God is a theological heresy.' The statement goes on to dissociate its authors from the racially motivated teachings and practices of other parts of the Christian community: 'Apartheid fails the test of the central biblical message of reconciliation. A few biblical texts, notably Genesis 11:1-9 and Acts 17:26, cannot save the situation. Wherever racialism is built into the structure of church and society, it is a denial of the common humanity of the believers and this in turn is a denial of the reconciling and humanising work of Christ.'

It is not new to say that the ideal Christian aim is to build a society which accepts and glorifies the differences between the races without making a barrier of them. In international terms, the aim is harmonious co-existence. Where different races are found within one national boundary, the aim is integration, not assimilation. Integration permits an immigrant group to play a full and responsible role in society without loss of cultural or national identity. Assimilation, on the other hand, is the process whereby such a group becomes submerged or absorbed into society so that its cultural heritage is totally destroyed.

Most people seem ready to agree that racialism is immoral but rarely do they say why it is so. Perhaps race relations could be helped if what seems to be a vague, inarticulate aversion to racial discrimination became instead a worked-out, explicitly grounded belief. Our hand will be strengthened if we establish clearly the principles from which we work.

On what grounds then does the Christian take his stand against racialism? It has been said that what makes Christian ethics Christian is its Christ-centredness summed up in phrases like 'following Christ' or 'the imitation of Christ'. So our attitude to the issue of race will seek to imitate that of Christ. Jesus was a Jew. But, as a member of that intensely nationalistic race, he rose above its narrowness and exclusivism, thereby incurring the anger and enmity of his fellow-countrymen. His sermon at Nazareth stressed that God's grace reaches further than the Jews like to think: 'But in truth, I tell you, there were many widows in Israel . . . and Elijah was sent to none of them but only to . . . the land of Sidon' (Luke 4:25, 26, *RSV*).

It is 'the world' to which Jesus came to bring light (John 8:12) and the same is true for his disciples (Matthew 5:14). Also, in the parable of the weeds among the wheat, the field is said to be 'the world' (Matthew 13:38). Even the focal point of Jewish worship, the Temple itself, is to be 'for all the nations' (Mark 11:17, *RSV*). Similarly, the command was given to 'make disciples of all nations' (Matthew 28:19, *RSV*). In these words there is no hint that any one race is either superior or inferior to another. Indeed, the reverse is true. All nations are to receive the gospel, a gospel sounding its keynote of reconciliation.

Colin Morris has described his experiences as a naïve expatriate minister of religion in southern Africa in his compelling book, *The Hour after Midnight* (Longmans, 1961). He was minister of a 'white', city church and suddenly realised he was imbibing unconsciously the rationalisations, the racialist attitudes and assumptions of the white population generally. He ransacked his Scriptures for new light. He writes: 'The book of Genesis makes it clear that God set his stamp and image upon all men as the fundamental ground of their equality. He did not select certain races for this honour. . . . There is no biblical justification for assuming that those of God's children with white skins have the dignity of divine creations unconditionally, whilst those with black skins must prove their worthiness before that dignity is extended to them.' Morris turned to the New Testament: 'In the New Testament I was utterly astonished at the claim that anyone who can utter with sincerity the invocation "Our Father", is thereby admitted to one great family circle, to be equal sharer in the inexhaustible parental love of God and equally entitled to all the privileges and responsibilities of family life.'

> *Join hands then, brothers of the faith,*
> *What'er your race may be;*
> *Who serves my Father as a son*
> *Is surely kin to me*
>
> (John Oxenham)

Having seen where the unambiguous emphasis in Scripture lies, we ask now how Christian teaching, shaped as doctrine, offers help. Whilst imitative in character, Christian ethics is essentially theological. Christian behaviour is conditioned by Christian beliefs, or ought to be. Allowing doctrine to determine, albeit indirectly, our actions is sometimes called 'having the courage of our convictions'! So which Christian doctrines affect our thinking about race relations?

We need not look far. 'In the beginning' God created the heavens and the earth and said 'Let us make man in our image, after our likeness' (Genesis 1:26). Here 'man' means 'mankind', the entire human species without exception. Of all the creatures, only man is made in God's image. All men are equal in their freedom to disobey the divine will and equal in their responsibility before God. Every man, whatever his race, bears the divine image. In the New Testament Paul calls man 'the image and glory of God' (1 Corinthians 11:7) and in passages like Matthew 25:40-45 we meet the concept of the Christ in every man. Inasmuch as the racialist unjustly discriminates against a member of another race, he discriminates against Christ.

Closely linked with the Christian doctrine of creation is the Christian doctrine of man which teaches that all men are equal in intrinsic worth. There are differences of course. But these are God-given and therefore good. 'God saw everything that he had made, and, behold, it was very good' (Genesis 1:31). In the dispensation of Christ, potential barriers between men are reduced to trivialities for 'there is neither Jew nor Greek, there is neither slave nor free, there is neither male nor female' (Galatians 3:28). Above all, each and every member of the human race stands in need of grace. There is none free from sin and without a need to be forgiven. Grace deprives a man of any claim to status.

This brings us to the doctrine of the atonement. Sin requires forgiveness which results in reconciliation. The reconciliation of man with God must lead to the reconciliation of man with man. Segregation on racial grounds denies a gospel of reconciliation. Is there a man for whom Christ did not die? Does Christ love some men more than others? Questions like these need acted, not spoken, answers. Let the loving and accepting relationships of salvationists around the world be a living testimony to the victory of Christ the universal reconciler.

This does not mean we have to become 'black' with white skins or become 'white' with black skins. We have to remain essentially ourselves, but made over anew in Jesus and thereby offering unconditional acceptance to those not of our own race. The other's culture in particular will be respected—respected, not necessarily embraced or indeed enjoyed. Even in forms of worship there may have to be a recognition that one cultural pattern of religious

41

activity holds little appeal for those accustomed to something very different. At the same time, there will be a mutual willingness to share with and to learn from those unlike ourselves.

Salvationists, with strong doctrine, but with strong, compassionate understanding of the fears that racial differences can so easily arouse, have tried, all over the world, with varying degrees of success, to provide the 'acted, not spoken, answers' called for above. These answers have often been on a personal level, less often on a national, political scale. The Army has been glad through the years to be free to evangelise and to meet material human need even in those lands where the government of the day is less than Christian, less than evenhanded in its treatment of all its citizens. But there always comes a point where the wounds and sorrows of some victimised section of humanity must be protested against. Politics, in its general sense of the life of the people in the community, cannot be avoided. We would agree, however, with Trevor Huddleston *(Naught for your Comfort)* when he states: 'Whilst I believe profoundly in the prophetic office of the church, I do not believe at all in political predictions. Whilst I would in any company defend the right of the church to take part in the political life of the country, I would deny as categorically its right to align itself with any one party. Great men of God, the Old Testament prophets, would simply not have thought of asking, "Can we get involved in politics?", for the words God gave them to speak were always directed at society in the totality of its life. Personal piety, corporate piety is good, but not enough. True spirituality takes God's people into issues and conflicts which are costly.' We need only mention William and Bramwell Booth and W. T. Stead to be reminded of the early-day Army's readiness to take on evil at whatever the cost.

However, we would not accept the claims of what has come to be known as liberation theology. With its roots in Latin America and through the pens of Christian men like Gustavo Gutierrez *(A Theology of Liberation)* and Miguez Bonino *(Doing Theology in a Revolutionary Situation)* it has come to equate the spiritual salvation offered in Christ with political freedom, even if it has to be achieved by revolutionary and violent means. The advocates of liberation theology have often demonstrated their willingness to meet the demands of self-sacrifice and more than one has felt the stern weight of some Latin American authority as he has visibly aligned himself with the oppressed. Admiration for such spirit ought not to blind us to the unjustified assertions of the theology, which tends to promote Marxist economics in place of saving faith in Jesus, Son of God. But if liberation theology relegates grace, it presents a compelling challenge to those who say personal piety is enough.

Racialism is contrary to God's will for man whether the racialist is black or white. F. B. Welbourn, writing in *The Expository Times,* sums it up this way: 'To say, "I am black", "I am white"—to say even, "I am a Christian", if that is to be a member of an exclusive group—is false because it is less than the truth and dangerously hides the truth that, in Christ, we are simply men.'

8

Warfare

MOST of this chapter is given over to a description of the 'just war' doctrine, which has been the backbone of Christianity's response to international violence for several centuries. First, however, a clear distinction should be made between the idea of a just war and that of a so-called 'holy' war. The latter plays no part in modern Christian thinking on the ethical problems raised by warfare for in a 'holy' war, such as the crusades, the enemy was seen as demonic, not human, and therefore not only liable to be killed but positively deserving of death. Such an enemy was regarded as evil personified, to whom no mercy could be shown, no quarter given and certainly no honourable burial accorded. Conversely, in conflicts where the enemy was not infidel but Christian (at least nominally) his dead would be given a Christian, perhaps even sorrowful, burial.

The 'just war' doctrine presupposes the humanity of all the peoples of the earth, whether Christians or not. It sought to replace the 'holy' war idea with checks and restraints upon those circumstances in which the state might with justification: *(a)* initiate a war; *(b)* conduct that war.

The doctrine grew up as an attempt to demonstrate when the evil of war might be endured in preference to some even greater evil of injustice or oppression. Some ridicule the doctrine by saying it is but a ploy on the part of warmongers to cloak with respectability their desire to engage in violence for whatever reason. This, however, is to distort the truth. The 'just war' concept, until modern times, has been seen as a limiting factor on large-scale violence; not an excuse, but a restrainer.

Before outlining the doctrine, something must be said about the way the New Testament is often used when Christians debate the ethics of war. Non-pacificists and pacifists alike (there are salvationists in both categories) claim to find support in Scripture

44

for their particular view. Matthew 5:38-48 is often seen as binding Christians to an absolute policy of non-violence, whatever the circumstances. At the turn of the century, Robert E. Speer commented on this view as follows: 'Jesus does enjoin brotherly love and long-suffering, but he does not thereby mean to secure to injustice a perfectly free field when it has power to work its will. The position of some opponents of war reduces itself to this, that bad men may resist bad men, but good men may not. Jesus did not teach this view' *(The Principles of Jesus)*.

It seems plain that Christians are called to resist evil. The issue arises over the means to be adopted. So the relevant question is: 'Is war ever a legitimate means by which Christians may resist evil?' In Romans 13 the apostle Paul clearly recognised that governments (as over against private citizens) have not only a right but a positive duty to resist evil by the sword. It is futile to argue that this applies only to non-Christian governments. To quote Speer once more: 'It is not possible that God should intend a heathen government to prevent evil, but a Christian government to permit it.'

When discussing the teaching of Jesus, it is a mistake to inject into his words a legality not intended when they were first spoken. He lays down principles, not rules. He advocated turning the other cheek (Matthew 5:39), but in John 18:22 there is no hint that he offered his other cheek when struck unjustly. Furthermore, the gospels frequently tell us how he took active steps to avoid capture and death until the occasion was right for him to submit. The principle by which Jesus seemed to have acted therefore is: 'Resist when it is right to resist, but submit when it is right to submit.' This is certainly how the advocates of the 'just war' doctrine have interpreted his teaching. They say that the Christian is committed to peace but he strives for other social goals as well. We seek justice, security and freedom. If we give peace an absolute priority whatever the circumstances, it will sometimes mean that exploitation and oppression go freely on their way.

Thomas Aquinas (see also Chapter Six) was a 13th-century Italian monk whose influence upon theology and philosophy continues to the present day. He sets out his theory of the 'just war' in his *Summa Theologica,* relying heavily on the views of Augustine. According to Aquinas, the foremost factor in a 'just war' is that it must be initiated by proper authority of the sovereign. War is not for private citizens to wage. Secondly, there must be sufficient cause for the war. That is, an enemy may be attacked if he deserves it. Aquinas adopts Augustine's definition of a 'just cause': 'One that avenges wrongs, when a nation or state has to be punished for refusing to make amends for wrongs inflicted by its subjects, or to restore what it has seized unjustly.' Thirdly, a just war is one waged with a 'good intention'. The intention must be to secure the common good and ultimately to bring about peace. Aquinas says that even if a war is waged by the right authority and for a just cause, it will be unjust if the intention behind it is wicked.

The aim of this theory, as stressed already, is to place limitations upon the waging of war. Aquinas argues that there is something essentially unchristian in shedding blood, even in a just war. But he accepts the necessity of sometimes having to resist a greater evil by means of the lesser evil of fighting a just war.

After Aquinas there was little development in the 'just war' doctrine until the 16th century and the rise of the great nation-states. The work of Francisco de Vitoria (1480-1546) and Francisco Suarez (1548-1617) paved the way for that of Hugo Grotius, a Dutch jurist born in 1583 and sometimes hailed as 'the father of international law'. In his treatise, *On the Law of War and Peace,* he starts by assuming that a thing is lawful for a Christian if it is not unjust. He says that he finds no clear teaching in the gospels about war and so he argues from general principles: 'The courage which defends our country from barbarians abroad, or the helpless from harm at home, or society from robbers, is complete justice.' He agrees with Aquinas that war is essentially inhuman and that only the 'highest necessity' or the 'deepest charity' could justify it.

Discussing pacifism, Grotius says that each man has an absolute right of conscientious objection so that, even in a just war, any Christian unwilling to fight should be excused. He saw it as particularly holy to abstain from lawful military service. He argued that it is more pious (in the best sense of the word) to give up our rights even if we would be justified in going to war. He adds, however, that this does not mean that it would be blameworthy to assert our rights and enter upon a just war in the same circumstances. Feelings can run high on this matter of conscientious objection. The Army's formal position was spelt out in a short official statement in 1980:

The Salvation Army respects the right of the individual to arrive at his own decision on the question of bearing arms in military service, based on personal Christian conviction, without seeking to influence any individual in either direction. The Army offers a full spiritual ministry to those arriving at either decision, with all possible help and guidance.

Based on scriptural teaching concerning respect for properly consti-tuted civil authority, the Army counsels those who object to military service to accept the legal means provided for alternative service, where such exists.

In no circumstances does the Army regard a sincere conscientious objector with any sense of stigma. It sees any such attitude as being a negation of the love of the Lord Jesus Christ, whose power alone can enable men to learn to live together in peace.

Hugo Grotius dealt not only with the question of when it is right for a Christian to go to war but also with that of how a just war ought to be conducted. Two main principles emerge, the principles of discrimination and proportion. The former seeks to protect non-combatants from direct attack. It maintains that military action should discriminate between directly attacking combatants and non-combatants. This is not the same, however, as saying that civilians should never knowingly be killed. It is a question of one's primary target. However, great difficulty may arise in deciding who is and who is not a combatant. The usual test is to decide whether a person is engaged in war, war preparation or war threat. If the answer is yes, then the person is a combatant, otherwise a non-combatant. But even the idea of being 'engaged in war' is a loose one. This might be said of a child who buys war stamps or writes notes of encouragement to his elder brothers in the armed forces or carries sandwiches to his father working in the munitions factory. Barrie Paskins and Michael Dockrill in their admirable analysis of the 'just war' theory, *The Ethics of War* (Duckworth, 1979), suggest that a combatant should be defined as a person who is *(a)* engaged in activity which has a military dimension which *(b)* is an activity which adds meaning to the person's life. By this test the growers of food (whether or not described as 'digging for victory') are non-combatants since growing food does not have a military dimension. The child buying war stamps is a non-combatant, but his father building munitions is a combatant and so too is the person who farms by day but fights, guerilla style, by night.

The principle of proportion requires that only those means should be used which are a necessary precondition of achieving the end in view. If an enemy can be stopped by some means short of killing, then that means is the one to adopt because it involves the lesser evil. The end justifies the means (since nothing else can!)—but not any means. This is an attempt to restrict to a necessary minimum the wounds inflicted and the lives lost. It is good theory, but elusive practice. Can anyone in a war see the overall picture? Has anyone a sense of proportion? The task of ensuring that from hour to hour, month to month, no excesses take place is extremely difficult. However, the concept is still widely accepted as relevant to morality in the midst of war. The media still pick up stories of 'atrocities' perpetrated in battle which are beyond

47

the limits of fair play. These atrocities, let us remember, are over and above the atrocity of the war itself.

If the principles of discrimination and proportion are still regarded as fundamental to the moral conduct of a war, it is increasingly difficult to see how they can always be applied to modern warfare. The line between combatants and non-combatants, as we have seen, is blurred. In the Second World War the two basic principles of discrimination and proportion were virtually abandoned. The obliteration bombing of Dresden on the one hand and London and Coventry on the other bears witness to this fact. The actions were aimed directly at civilians and were inordinately excessive. This trend away from traditional thinking is encouraged by the advent of atomic and nuclear devices which have to be used without the ability to select pin-point targets. They are 'all or nothing' weapons. Henry Nelson Wieman was right to say that the first atomic explosion 'cut history in two like a knife'.

One especially difficult problem today facing not only Christian moralists but moralists in general is to work out an ethic for counter-insurgency warfare. What has the Christian to say about the morality of the means employed in fighting terrorists in, for instance, Northern Ireland? The terrorist fights from behind or amongst the civilian population. His is a subversive war. He hits and runs. He thinks it is better to strike and run away and live to fight another day. So far his tactics have succeeded. The United Kingdom has frequently been stunned by callous bombings of innocent citizens by terrorists. Many have lost their lives and many more have been injured. No country is immune. How then is it possible to mount a morally acceptable counter-terrorist operation when sometimes the enemy is a child with a bomb or a housewife with a shotgun?

We have space here only to ask the question and thereby highlight the issue. It is an issue of some importance for our time. The 'just war' doctrine and its precepts seem of limited practical help in combating terrorism. Must we then sink to the tactics of the terrorist and reply in kind? Answers are urgently needed and Christians are as obliged as anyone else to provide them. The Church is all too often accused of failing to give a clear moral lead. But modern insurgency warfare is one area in which answers do not easily present themselves.

What at least is clear is that Christians must seek and support the peaceful settlement of disputes whenever it is possible. We must oppose those who reject the relevance of spiritual factors when it comes to policy making. Equally, we must oppose those who are unrealistic enough to ignore completely the material considerations. And we must never forget to uphold against all other claims the vocation of those who renounce violence even in the highest cause. Such souls may not constitute the loaf, but we should fear the day when they are no longer allowed to be the leaven.

We go on now to look more closely at warfare with a nuclear dimension.

9

Nuclear warfare (1)

SOONER or later, there dawns the realisation in every man's mind that one day he will die. Men learn to live with this. What we have not learned to live with is the dawning realisation that one day man as a species may die. It is a generation since the advent of the thermo-nuclear bomb, but is that long enough to work out an ethic for the invention, possession, threatened use and actual use of nuclear weapons? For those of pacifist conviction weapons of mass destruction will be regarded in the same light as any other instrument of violence, that is, as morally reprehensible. For those who do not share a pacifist view, and who would accept that in certain limited circumstances war is justified as the lesser of two evils, it is a question of deciding whether the traditional criteria for determining the justness of a war can be made to apply to war carried on by nuclear means. Opinion on this question, even in Christian circles, is sharply divided.

Over several centuries Christian thinkers have evolved principles designed to limit the circumstances in which war might be waged against an enemy. These principles are enshrined in the doctrine of the just war (see Chapter Eight). Many commentators claim that events during the Second World War revealed the total inadequacy of the just war doctrine for modern warfare. The technology of international violence, it is said, has outstripped Christian ethical thinking when it comes to war. This is because the principle of discrimination, which seeks to protect non-combatants, has been repeatedly flouted, in the Second World War and since. If these commentators are right, then the just war concept cannot be adequate for the age of nuclear weapons of mass and indiscriminate destruction. Many moral theologians have now thrown over the just war doctrine as totally irrelevant for our times; instead they seek a code of ethics for the possession and potential use of nuclear weapons. Such an approach would seem to this writer to be fallacious. There are impulses in the lower nature of man which can render him a creature of unmatched ferocity. These impulses have been held in check for many generations (or at least partly in check) by an insistence on adherence to the doctrine of the just war. If modern technology has taken us well beyond our former capacities for inflicting harm upon our fellows we ought not to be changing our ethics to fit the technology, but throwing out the technology to fit the well-tried ethical safeguards. The doctrine outlined in the last chapter is imperfect both in theory and in application, but as yet we have nothing better to put in its place and, certainly, we shall rue the day we allow it to decline in favour of nuclear fatalism.

How the weapons came

On 2 August 1939 Albert Einstein warned the President of the United States of America, Franklin D. Roosevelt, that the country was engaged in scientific research into nuclear fission with far-reaching implications for warfare. The research was being conducted at the University of Chicago under the supervision of Julius Oppenheimer. By 1943 fission had been achieved, plus a detonation technique and a means of successfully enclosing that technique in a conventional bomb casing. On 12 April 1945, President Roosevelt died to be succeeded by President Truman. The new president was totally ignorant of the research being carried out and only on taking office did he realise that the United States was perfecting an explosive device great enough to destroy the world.

In July 1945 the first test was carried out in the Mexican desert. A ball of plutonium the size of a grapefruit was set on a tower 100 feet high. The experimenters retired to a safe distance of 11 miles and detonated the plutonium. An explosion ensued equivalent to that which would have been caused by 20,000 tons of TNT. A crater 1,200 feet wide was produced and all living organisms within it ceased instantly to exist. Iron pipes four inches thick within the crater were immediately vaporised. At the moment of detonation, ground temperature was 100 million °F. This is three times hotter than the estimated temperature at the core of the sun or 10,000 times hotter than the estimated temperature of the sun's surface. Can man, such awful power placed in his hands, be trusted to use it aright?

The men in the Mexican desert were the first to see the satanic mushroom cloud.

It is now simply a matter of record that on 6 August 1945 an American pilot dropped the first nuclear device on the Japanese

51

city of Hiroshima. The era of conventional weapons had ended and the balance of terror had begun. The bomb over Hiroshima was detonated at a height of 2,000 feet. Ninety thousand buildings were destroyed including 26 fire stations and 42 hospitals. Of the 298 doctors in the city, 270 were killed. To stand even a 50 per cent chance of survival the inhabitants would have to have been one-and-a-half miles from the epi-centre of the explosion. It has been estimated that the number of total instant deaths was between 90,000 and 250,000. A similar fate befell Nagasaki on 9 August 1945. Death on these two occasions was caused primarily by blast from the explosion, that is, air displacement creating winds up to a speed of 160 mph and, of course, radiation subsequent to the explosion. Even today, Japanese citizens are still dying as a result of the effects of radioactive fallout following the attacks of 1945.

In August 1949, the USSR exploded its own atom bomb, commencing the arms race 'spiral'. Since then, peace has rested not on mutual trust but on mutual terror. In 1960, the ill-fated President John F. Kennedy said the world contained 30 billion tons of TNT—10 tons per human being. By 1978, the United States had enough nuclear power to destroy each Soviet city of 100,000 people or more 41 times over. Conversely, the Soviet Union could destroy each American city of 100,000 persons or more 23 times over. In nuclear parlance this is known as overkill.

The classic claim made in defence of nuclear weapons is that their existence has ensured peace for the last 40 years. But have they? Since the end of 1945 more lives have been lost in conflict than both world wars. In the light of this, claims for nuclear weapons are watered down, and it is said that their existence has deterred, if not conventional war, then nuclear war. This is an absurd, circular argument.

The first nuclear weapons were massive and totally indiscriminate in that any hope of targetting them accurately was vain. It was the era of MAD or Mutually Assured Destruction when nuclear nations knew for sure that a first strike would end with the initiator, as well as the recipient, annihilated. It should be noted, however, that times change and we are no longer in even the first or second generation of nuclear weapons. We live now in the age of the neutron bomb which kills people by radiation and has a minimum blast effect. This weapon has been produced by the USA and, in June 1983, successfully tested, but not produced, by France. A neutron bomb can be used with much greater precision than its nuclear predecessor, thus limiting the effect upon civilian members of the population. Mutual Assured Destruction has gone and we have moved into an era in which the possibility of a limited

52

nuclear war becomes ever more distinct. There are those who would claim that this will happen in our lifetime. No longer does a state possess nuclear weapons in order to deter a potential enemy from taking a first nuclear strike against it. The primary purpose today of nuclear weapons is to deter *any* attack against you, even an attack by conventional means. It is no longer the case that nuclear weapons would be used only in the overall context of an exclusively nuclear exchange. Instead, we have now the concept of the 'flexible response' by which the powers belonging to the North Atlantic Treaty Organisation (NATO) would be prepared to use nuclear weapons to repel (for example) a Soviet incursion into Western Europe by means of conventional tank weapons. This concept has made nuclear war more 'thinkable' than ever before. Indeed, governments now simply assume the feasibility of a limited nuclear war. No longer is such a war seen as unwinnable. The era of MAD may have gone, but madness, apparently, has not. The concept of a limited, winnable nuclear conflict is the most dangerous confronting the nations today.

The weapons today

Those countries with nuclear arsenals of their own are the USA, the Soviet Union, France and Great Britain. It is suspected that Israel, Iraq, Pakistan, India and South Africa either have, or shortly will have, some sort of nuclear capacity. The information available to the writer relates primarily to nuclear weapons held in Britain. Britain has her own independent nuclear deterrent which is part of the NATO strategy, but she hosts other NATO forces. Her nuclear weapons are both tactical (short-range) and strategic (long-range). At the time of writing (1984) the following are the weapons:
Polaris: Britain has four nuclear submarines equipped with 16 Polaris missiles each. These missiles have a range of 2,880 miles. Each warhead divides into three and each has a yield of 200 kilotons (compared with the 13 kilotons at Hiroshima). Polaris missiles lack accuracy but if one hit a city centre it would kill 250,000 people.
The Chevaline System: Mr Francis Pym, when he was Secretary of State for Defence, announced that this system would be used to modernise the existing Polaris system so that the missile could be manoeuvred between firing and detonation.
Trident: In the long-term, this will replace the Polaris submarine system. By the 1990s, Britain will have purchased from the United States several submarines each of which will be the length of two soccer fields, the height of a five-storey building, the bearer of 24

53

ballistic missiles each carrying 14 warheads. The range will be in excess of 4,000 miles. One Trident submarine, fully armed, can destroy 192 cities.

The Buccaneer: There are 60 Buccaneer strike aircraft, each with a range of 500 miles and each carrying two warheads. They are thought to be highly vulnerable to enemy air-defence forces, or to a knock-out strike on an air base.

NATO Nuclear Forces based in Britain: There are 170 F-111 bombers stationed in Britain which are owned and operated by the United States. The nuclear warheads for these are provided under 'dual-key' arrangements which means that the co-operation of both Britain and the United States is necessary if the weapons are to be used. Towards the end of 1979, as a pre-arms reduction talks tactic, NATO decided to deploy 464 Cruise missiles in Europe. Some 160 of these will be based at Greenham Common, Berkshire, and at Molesworth in Cambridgeshire. Deployment began at the end of 1983 (to be completed by 1988) and as a result the Soviet Union walked out of the Geneva talks on intermediate nuclear forces (not to be confused with similar talks on strategic nuclear arms). Also in 1979, NATO decided to deploy 108 Pershing II ballistic missiles throughout Europe. However, on 23 July 1982 the first new Pershing II missile was tested at the Kennedy Space Centre in the United States where it exploded shortly after take-off showering debris into the Atlantic. It was not carrying a nuclear warhead at the time. Problems remain to be overcome if it is to be deployed on schedule. The British government have reluctantly admitted there is no physical 'dual-key' arrangement for either Cruise or Pershing, but insists that assurances have been given that no USA weapons based in the UK would be used unless the British government first assented. Just how such assent is to be sought and given with Soviet missiles only four minutes away is not made clear. Finally, Britain plays host to a handful of US Poseidon submarines each of which carries 16 missiles, each missile having 10 warheads.

How a nuclear war might start

Firstly, a nuclear war could start by mistake. The nations frequently engage in 'war games'. Such exercises carried on without disconnecting the alert systems could result in disaster. Then again, the role of computers and silicone chips in the control of nuclear weapons means that a faulty silicone chip could see a Cruise missile launched in error and Cruise missiles are unrecallable. A nuclear accident is not a possibility to be sneered at. Figures released by the Stockholm International Peace Research Institute indicate that before 1968 there were not less than 33 major US accidents involving total loss of, or damage to, a nuclear device. It is known that on at least five separate occasions a US missile has overshot its target and crashed near foreign soil, one landing close to Cuba in 1967. In October 1960, there was the famous incident in which the North American Air Defence Command thought that it had received early warning from Greenland of a missile attack on the United States of America. It took 15 minutes for it to be realised that the American radar systems had simply echoed off the moon!

Secondly, a nuclear war could begin as the result of a deliberate act of aggression. One possibility is of a minor power without warning launching a nuclear attack on a traditional enemy. Alternatively, there must be a very strong temptation indeed for a major power to take the initiative of a first strike despite all the public statements that such a step would never be undertaken.

But with the woes of sin and strife
The world has suffered long;
Beneath the angel-strain have rolled
Two thousand years of wrong.
And man, at war with man, hears not
The love song which they bring;
O hush the noise, ye men of strife,
And hear the angels sing.
Edmund Hamilton Sears

10

Nuclear warfare (2)

THIS chapter seeks to show what havoc may be wreaked by nuclear devices, but thereafter to show possible causes for Christian hope. First, however, let us remember the more subtle effects upon our communities of the mere possession of nuclear weapons.

To contemplate a nuclear conflict within our own lifetime is, for most of us, to think the unthinkable. What parent amongst us has not pondered his sleeping child and tried to guess whether that young life will end prematurely in instantaneous vaporisation or, even worse perhaps, will drain away in the lingering throes of radiation sickness? But it is not only the parent who harbours secret thoughts. Today's child does not have to be very old before he becomes aware of the awful possibility of a world-consuming nuclear conflagration. It is slowly being acknowledged that hitherto undetected and virtually unmeasurable damage is being done to our young people by the psychological climate created by the suggestion that we must accept as morally justifiable the obliteration of the world we know. In 1962, D. M. MacKinnon, Professor of Divinity in the University of Cambridge, said, 'None who have had any measure of responsibility for the pastoral care of young people can remain oblivious to the extent to which these issues press upon the minds of the most sensitive.' He was referring to the moral issues involved in the existence and possible use of nuclear weapons.

Children in the 1980s are no less sensitive. Even when they do not discuss the issues with their parents, they debate them with teachers for the possibility of nuclear war weighs heavily upon the minds of teenagers. There arises therefore a duty upon parents and Christian leaders to be informed and articulate about the whole question, and in turn to inform and render articulate those young people within their care. Many have found that the most effective way of coming to terms with the matter is simply to be well informed about it and to think it through calmly and responsibly. To this there are two alternatives: ignorance or panic.

What the weapons do

During the month of September 1981, there appeared on American television screens a CBS series, 'The Defence of the United States', which began with a simulation of a 15-megaton nuclear attack on the strategic air command near Omaha, Nebraska. The film predicted a fireball at ground level for 20 seconds and a crater three-and-a-quarter miles across. The fireball would rise to 80,000 feet in less than a minute, and people 16 miles away would suffer second and third-degree burns. Some 35 miles away, people giving a reflex glance at the explosion would be blinded by retinal burning. There would be skull fractures, ruptured lungs, crushing injuries to the thorax, broken backs, deep lacerations and haemorrhages. Even 12 miles away, the pressure would be enough to shatter windows into lethal slivers of glass propelled at 100 mph. With petrol stations and main services likely to be set alight, a fire storm could burn for up to eight hours at 800°C. Apart from the dead, there would be at least 200,000 seriously injured persons and the number of these with third-degree burns would easily exceed the total number (2,000) of intensive care burn beds in the whole of the United States. After six weeks the total dead would be well in excess of two million. Commenting on this series during an interview on BBC Television, Dr Jack Geiger, Professor of Community Medicine at the City College, New York, said that American nuclear shelters would be useless in such circumstances. He claimed that a 15-megaton attack would dry-roast people in shelters and cremate them, even where the shelters were three storeys deep underground.

Here in Britain, there are as yet few fall-out shelters. The official civil defence effort so far amounts to little more than advising the population to stay put and make themselves rudimentary shelters from living-room doors placed at an angle against interior walls of the house!

It is precarious to seek to predict with any accuracy the effects of a nuclear attack. So much will depend on the number of devices used, the density of the population, the height above the ground at which the explosion occurs, the prevailing weather conditions, the time of year and the amount of warning given before the attack. It is true that some effects are common to any nuclear attack, that is, blast and radiation, but there will in all probability be effects not yet contemplated.

The major causes of death will be burns from heat radiation, being crushed in buildings destroyed by blast, colliding with objects in the high winds produced by the blast, receiving lethal doses of radiation from fall-out and being burned in fires. For those who survive in the first instance, their chances of ultimate recovery from burns will be seriously reduced if they have also been exposed to radiation, since such exposure significantly reduces the capacity of one's body in blood replacement.

Calculated effects

If we take an example of a one-megaton nuclear explosion in a built-up area, the blast and heat effects have been calculated as follows: the wall of an average two-storey house four miles from the explosion would be subjected to a force of more than 180 tons, and a wind of 160 mph would create fatal collisions not only between people and impelled objects, but between people and people. There would be a two-second flash of heat radiation travelling at the speed of light. It would cause third-degree burns on people exposed to the flash up to a distance of five miles. Such burns would destroy the skin and if received on more than 24 per cent of the body would certainly be fatal unless prompt specialised medical care was available. A solitary nuclear weapon could produce at least 10,000 such patients. The whole of the United States, as has been shown, has facilities to treat no more than 2,000 cases of severe burns.

The foregoing seeks to describe the short-term damage. The long-term effects would consist of radiation-induced cancer and genetic damage to future generations. The inevitable breakdown of normal civic and domestic amenities would produce unimagined shortages of food and medical facilities. Disease and starvation would be rife. Official government documents exist in Britain which predict that after a nuclear attack it would be necessary to invoke on-the-spot executions for any person found stealing food.

In June 1981 the Royal Swedish Academy of Sciences completed a two-year project designed to determine the possible consequences of a large-scale nuclear holocaust in the northern hemisphere. These findings were published in *Ambio,* the official journal of the academy. A nuclear battle was assumed to have taken place on one June morning in 1985. The weather was average for June. The journal reports that 750 million people, roughly half of the population of the cities of the northern hemisphere, where the bombing would be concentrated, would die within 24 hours of the exchange, due to blast, radiation burns and fire. A further 250 million would be destined to die within a few weeks or months from radiation sickness and the expected collapse of organised medical care. Over 75 per cent of the total population of the urban northern hemisphere would die in the battle or shortly after it. This would mean 1,000 million dead.

In a sense, these findings were predictable. Less familiar are the projected effects of nuclear weapons on the atmosphere. A leading chemist from West Germany, Doctor Paul Ciutzen, stated that forests would be set ablaze over 400,000 square miles. This would all take place within the space of a few days. These forest fires would throw 200 to 400 million tons of dust and smoke into an atmosphere already choked by oil and gas vapour from the destruction of wells and oil depots, and the total result would be a heavy dark cloud round the northern hemisphere which could blot out the sunlight for months. In other words, the chaos on the ground would be taking place in semi-darkness and agriculture would simply stop. Consequently, those who survived the immediate impact of the conflagration would die within a year of famine. Finally, even though the battle took place in the northern hemisphere, its impact would be felt in the southern hemisphere. Whilst the northern hemisphere has only 25 per cent of the world's population, it produces 60 to 65 per cent of the world's grain and most of the fertilisers. Without these items there would be a further 1,000 million to 3,000 million deaths from starvation in the south. The *Ambio* report concluded that from all of this it seemed far from certain that civilisation might rebuild itself.

Hope?

In November 1969, in the era of Richard Nixon and Henry Kissinger, there began the Strategic Arms Limitation Talks (SALT). After three years an agreement of sorts was reached between the United States and the Soviet Union on limiting nuclear arms production. On 29 June 1982 a new round of talks began in Geneva known as START (Strategic Arms Reduction Talks). Formerly the talks were about limitations, but now they are about actual reductions in the levels of nuclear stockpiles and this is to be welcomed. President Ronald Reagan proposed that both the USA and the Soviet Union reduce their warhead numbers by at least one-third so that both sides hold equal amounts. The Russians rejected the proposal as unfair. They suggested instead a freeze for the time being on all nuclear arms production including a suspension of any steps being taken to modernise existing systems. Despite the lack of agreement right at the outset of the talks, neither side appeared to be discouraged and the talks are going ahead. The American chief negotiator was Edward Rowny and his Soviet opposite number was Viktor Karpov.

The main hope for mankind in preventing nuclear catastrophe lies in reversing the nuclear spiral so that one day the world is one large nuclear-free zone. This will take a miracle. We know of one who specialises in miracles. By the grace of God we shall ponder the issues with courage and with calm resolution to think them through.

The first step is to work out our ethical position in relation to the state of affairs gripping the world in an iron fist today. The Christian will not be fooled into thinking that the issues are political only. The Holy Spirit will guide him to a recognition of the deep moral questions at the heart of the matter, questions such as: What may men do to one another? What may they do to the world into which they were born? Are there limits to a man's freedom of action? Can so-called public obligation always be accepted as a cover for morally dubious actions? Underlying any position finally adopted will be a Christian insistence that human affairs be humanely conducted, together with a Christian refusal to acquiesce in what we are told cannot be otherwise than it is. We should never forget that the thing in which we are bidden to acquiesce is man-made. What man has made, man can change.

Divided Christian opinion

Already Christian opinion in the matter has begun to divide. (See note at the end of this chapter.) Some believers offer ethical justifications for the possession of nuclear weapons. They defend the concept of deterrence and say that it is the duty of the government to deploy such weapons in defence of the population. Others go still further and declare that in certain circumstances even the positive use of nuclear weapons would be morally justified. They say that this would be so in the case of a limited nuclear exchange designed to forestall a large-scale exchange. Some Christians think these views are mistaken.

The basic choice which faces the Christian community is whether or not to go on using the just war doctrine as our guideline for what is or is not acceptable in terms of the international use of force. Either we dispense with the doctrine and retain nuclear military technology or we abide by the doctrine, grateful for its tried and tested principles, and act bravely as the consequences of it for nuclear weaponry become apparent.

We ought to be very slow to join those who brand the principles of the just war doctrine as archaic and irrelevant. If we bear in mind the twin foundations of discrimination and proportion it will be seen immediately that the indiscriminate use of weapons of mass destruction has to be immoral in all circumstances. Indeed, the entire weight of Christian thinking would support this. But what happens to our morality if the military leaders in an enemy state conceal themselves in an inner-city bunker surrounded by the mass of the civilian population? Would it be morally justified to target a nuclear warhead at the bunker knowing that it would inevitably destroy countless innocent lives in the same city? In reality, such a situation would not exist. No military leader would use merely a single missile for the task, since all the major cities would be protected by anti-ballistic missile systems. It would therefore be necessary to launch several missiles containing several warheads each against the offending bunker. Only by such means could it be ensured that at least one warhead would find its target. Other warheads would land where they might and the destruction would be vast. It simply is not plausible to think in terms of a limited and specific use of nuclear weapons along the lines suggested in the example above. Even if we think in terms of directing missiles at non-city targets, we still have to reckon with the risk of radioactive fall-out contaminating the atmosphere for hundreds of miles around and the same contamination being carried on the wind into densely inhabited regions. The plain fact is that *any* nuclear strike carries with it the fierce likelihood of massive loss of civilian life and a high risk of escalation to an all-out holocaust. Those who claim that a limited nuclear strike might sometimes be morally justified should instead recognise that a limited strike can be thought of only in the context of an ultimately all-embracing conflict. In other words, there is no such thing as a discriminating use of nuclear weapons.

However, even those who recognise that this is so sometimes claim that we ought to distinguish between using weapons and the mere possession or deployment of them. The argument is that it is morally acceptable to threaten to use them provided that you never actually press the button. There are difficulties with this position. It raises the question of whether or not it is immoral to intend to do an act which would be immoral if carried out in practice. The possession and threat are intended to deter the enemy from striking at you first, but the deterrent effect will bite only if the enemy believes absolutely that you intend to carry out your threat should the need to do so arise. Deterrence amounts to holding your enemy's entire civilian population as a hostage. This can never be morally acceptable. It simply will not do to argue that nuclear weapons are merely 'bluff' weapons, that they are 'weapons not to be used'. Granted that the Christian presenting such an argument is genuinely convinced of his own personal unwillingness to use the weapons were he in a position to take the decision, nevertheless he has to recognise that the commander of a Polaris submarine or pilot of a nuclear bomber or indeed the soldier trained as a missile-key operator will most certainly use the weapons if ordered to do so by his political leaders. Such people are trained and conditioned for precisely this eventuality. The distinction drawn between threatening to use and actually using such weapons is a false one.

Personal contribution

What can the individual Christian, who has no public influence or power, do to help? Here are some tentative suggestions:

1 Be as well-informed as possible. Our children often have the chance to discuss nuclear issues at school. How much better if they can discuss the issues and their feelings at home with knowledgeable parents.
2 Be calm and at peace within your soul by walking daily close to the Lord who loves you.
3 Be certain that, in the event of our worst fears being realised, you have something to offer a fear-paralysed neighbour. You cannot share what you do not possess, so let the foundations of your life go deep into Jesus.
4 Remember that whilst missiles can be dismantled, knowledge cannot be uninvented and so the human race has and will forever have the ability to destroy itself entirely in a short and measurable span of time.
5 Pray therefore for the leaders of nations. Pray for their military advisers. Pray for the peace talks negotiators and by name for the leaders of the Soviet and American delegations at the Geneva arms talks (Viktor Karpov and Max Kempelman). Prayer means the individual Christian, without political power, may influence events in accordance with God's will by praying in the name of and in the spirit of Jesus.
6 Refuse to see the presence of nuclear devices on our planet as inevitable. With the necessary political will, we can be rid of them—at a pace which retains international stability and balance.
7 Tell your children and grandchildren that the weapons can be dismantled and are not an inevitable fact of life.
8 Do not leave the thinking or the voicing of opinions only to the politicians. They need our help, our Christian help, to clarify the issues, especially the moral issues. There is no evidence that politicians, as a class, are more intelligent, wiser than or morally superior to any other comparable group.

9 Work on public opinion, not stridently but wisely, within your own circle of friends and contacts, gently but firmly promoting an abhorrence of nuclear weapons.

10 Contribute to peace by shunning strife in your personal relationships with family, friends and neighbours.

Theology in a nuclear age

Living in the nuclear age requires courage to face up to the awful possibilities for the future. We can pray to be granted courage, but let us pray also for God to raise up men and women with obedient Christian hearts and able Christian minds to give us a theology for a nuclear age.

What has the gospel to say to military generals in the late 20th century? What does Calvary mean to a polarised world, strangled by fear and mistrust? These and other similar questions are enormous in their implications. As we pray, and as we think, waiting upon God to guide, we can see again the crucial importance of the great Christian truths which will shape Christian nuclear theology between now and the next century:

1 God is alive, not dead. The God of Mount Carmel, the Red Sea, of Sinai, Bethlehem, Calvary and Pentecost is still able and willing to meet his people's need and to listen to their cry.

2 Jesus is risen, not dead. His spirit is set free in the world and men and women still, daily, yield to his Kingdom of forgiveness, love and grace.

3 Miracles happen. God is Lord of every molecule, every atom, every nucleus. He made them for our good and longs for us no longer to turn them to evil use.

4 The world is good. Creation is good. God has said so and has made us in his own likeness. To destroy God's creation, or even to threaten its destruction, is a blasphemy.

5 We are God's appointed stewards over the created order. We have a sacred responsibility toward our fellow man and the animals and plants. How is this discharged by littering the planet with devices of death?

6 The cross of Jesus speaks reconciliation, man to God and man to man, nation to God and nation to nation. We are God's agents in this reconciling work.

7 Jesus said that peacemakers are blessèd.

8 Genesis 9 contains the 'rainbow promise' that never again will God destroy the earth, and Matthew 24 promises salvation to those who, in war and rumours of war, endure faithfully in Christ until the end. There is no guarantee of physical safety, but there is an absolute promise that those who die in Christ, faithful to him, will be with him in all eternity.

63

When the theology has been worked out, and when the ethics have been expounded, there will yet be required of us two things: That our love for the Lord shall not wax cold even in the face of wars and rumours of wars, and that we shall never find ourselves unable or unwilling to discharge our sacred calling as salvationist evangelists and to offer to dying men and women not only pity, not only compassion, not only comfort, but the hope of eternity because of Christ who died first for them.

Most readers will know the book or the film of the story of Judah Ben Hur. Dreadful evil was perpetrated on him and his loved ones by alien occupiers of his native land. The wrongs they suffered were seemingly unforgiveable, and at last Ben Hur's chance for bloody vengeance came. He set out, bent on killing, sword in hand. Then he stumbled across an execution at Golgotha and heard the dying man say, 'Father, forgive them for they know not what they do.' Hatred drained away as Ben Hur heard dying words of love for sinful, ignorant men. Later, as he remembered, he said, *'I felt his words take the sword from my hand.'*

Hope in an armed world? Only in Jesus. Without him, we are running out of time.

Note

Below is a summary of recent official positions taken up by some Christian groups:

1 Pope John Paul II: In June 1982 he said that in current political conditions deterrence based on balance may still be judged morally acceptable, but only as a stepping-stone to total disarmament.

2 Church of England: In February 1983 the General Synod rejected the report of a working party, *The Church and The Bomb,* which advocated onesided (unilateralist) nuclear disarmament by Britain on moral grounds. The Synod approved, by 382 votes to 49 a resolution which allowed for: *(a)* the defensive possession of nuclear weapons; *(b)* international steps to reduce the number of nuclear weapons; *(c)* no first use, even on a small scale, by the UK. Archbishop Robert Runcie referred to 'the regrettable necessity of nuclear deterrence'.

3 The UK Free Church Federal Council: In April 1983 the Council, which represents (informally) some 13 free churches in England and Wales declared itself in favour of unilateral nuclear disarmament by Britain.

4 West Germany's Roman catholic bishops: In April 1983, after five years of thought, the bishops decided to tolerate nuclear deterrence, but not as a long-term strategy for peace. Deterrence, they said, must be but a step on the way to disarmament.

5   America's Roman catholic bishops: In May 1983, after two years of thought, called for a nuclear freeze and declared all nuclear war unwinnable. They reluctantly accepted the possession of nuclear devices for deterrence purposes but added that they should never be used.

6   United Reformed Church: In May 1983 the URC General Assembly, by 381 votes to 180, said, 'The non-conformist conscience does not feel that reliance on the deterrent, British or otherwise, is compatible with commitment to Christianity.'

7   The Quakers (Society of Friends): Their 1983 Yearly Meeting in Britain, held to formulate policy, resolved that quakers could withhold income tax in part, as a conscientious objection to war and defence policy.

8   Methodist Church: In June 1983 they declined to go unilateralist but backed a nuclear freeze. They decided to oppose the siting of Cruise or Pershing missiles in the UK, but only by 262 votes to 246 at their annual Conference.

9   The Salvation Army: In June 1983 General Jarl Wahlström issued a call to the United Nations and to world leaders to redouble efforts for peace and to divert funds from arms to alleviation of world poverty. The General's statement stressed greed and the desire to dominate as the sources of fear and tension in the world and reaffirmed God's love for all the peoples of the world. The General pledged that all salvationists would pray for peace. He called on the nations to positively reduce their total weapon capability to the absolute minimum and to cease production of nuclear devices and all associated machinery.

11

Pre-marital sex

EARLIER chapters in this book have indicated the Christian belief that the human capacity for sex is a lovely gift from God to mankind and that the right context for its use and expression is that of a life-long, exclusive commitment in marriage. This chapter attempts eventually to articulate the reason or reasons for the Christian attitude to pre-marital sex.

There is a great variety of activity which can be dubbed as 'pre-marital sex'. It ranges from prostitution to relations between couples engaged to be married, with many variations in between. Let us analyse some of these. It may help to enunciate a broad principle right at the beginning, a principle acceptable to all responsible persons, whether Christian or not. It was stated with eloquence and clarity earlier this century by Professor John Macmurray in *Reason and Emotion* (Faber, 1962 edition): 'The integrity of persons is inviolable. You shall not use a person for your own ends, or indeed for any ends, individual or social. To use another person is to violate his personality by making an object of him; and in violating the integrity of another, you violate your own.'

Prostitution, whether the prostitute is female or male, is the starkest instance of using another for self-gratification. Another's body is made available for money. Both parties may be entirely willing to enter the transaction but both are thereby degraded. There is no personal response. There may or may not be physical relief or gratification, but there is no love. The episode takes place on the biological plane alone. It is sadly animalistic. The Bible offers clear counsel in Proverbs 5 and 1 Corinthians 6:14-20.

Other casual encounters may take place without payment of money, but again the exchange consists merely in the realisation of sexual pleasure alone. There is no attendant personal involvement —indeed such involvement is expressly repudiated by the parties

66

who decline to accept responsibility for each other in any way. Promiscuity of this kind differs from prostitution only in the absence of payment. The conduct is again animalistic and if it is to be described justifiably as 'human' an involvement of more than bodies is necessary.

This brings us to transient encounters. These cannot be seen as single exchanges or as promiscuous since sexual intercourse may continue over a period of time as an expression of mutual liking or even friendship. However, the basis of the relationship is expressly transient. The two have come to know and like each other, but the understanding is clear—no commitment, no permanency and certainly no children. The relationship may eventually arouse in at least one of the parties a desire for permanency and, given the initial conditions for embarking on the adventure, jealousy and fear of loss will emerge. Dr Jack Dominian, renowned for his work and writings on sexual ethics and marriage, comments, 'Relationships are placed under a great strain when they have to live under the shadow of unilateral repudiation without any recourse or appeal to the contrary principle of continuity' (*Proposals for a New Sexual Ethic,* Darton, Longman and Todd, 1977). Transient sexual relationships mean permanent uncertainty about the future. Whilst marriage cannot guarantee the future, it does mean a mutual commitment to make every effort to defeat obstacles in the way of love growing to full maturity.

Next on the ladder of pre-marital sexual involvement come trial marriages. Some couples refrain from sexual intercourse—and indeed from any sexual contact which may make intercourse virtually irresistible—until they are sure they want to live together. They call the living together a trial marriage, but of course there is no such thing. If it is a trial, it is not a marriage; if it is a marriage, it is not a trial. This arrangement suffers the same defects as transient encounters except that now there is a distinct possibility of the relationship resulting in marriage, provided certain conditions are first satisfied. Each party in effect says to the other, 'If you pass the trial, I will probably agree to marry you.' They overlook the fact that there is no substitute for marriage and so their experiment is being carried out on the false premise that merely living under the same roof and sleeping together amounts to a simulation of the married state. Moreover, sex is not at its most satisfying, particularly for a woman, when performance is being assessed. In marriage, two lives are shared without reserve. It is a way of life not susceptible of 'trial'. You either enter into it or you leave it alone. Hugh Montefiore, in his contribution to *God, Sex and War* (Fontana, 1963) says, 'For a fiancé to try out his betrothed like a new hat or a new car to see whether he is likely to go on wanting her is to treat a fiancée like a thing and not a person. The trial is judged a failure unless it is positively a success; and under such circumstances it can hardly succeed.'

Having mentioned various types of pre-marital sexual exchange, we can look at the arguments which have been advanced against them.

First, and this ends the argument for some people, fornication is prohibited repeatedly in Scripture (for instance, 1 Corinthians 6:13; Ephesians 5:3; 1 Thessalonians 4:1-8). The authority of biblical commands is recognised amongst Christians generally, but there should be some way of showing the reasonableness of the command in question. A blind or unthinking appeal to authority will not satisfy the enquiring teenager and an appeal to the authority of Scripture will cut no ice with the unbeliever. The standard set must be capable of justification.

Second, the risk of venereal disease which is inherent in casual sexual adventuring has been put forward as a deterrent. The risk is a very real one. However, not every sexual encounter before marriage results in such disease and so some other ground must be found on which to base our standard.

Third, there is the risk of pregnancy, even with the advent of contraception in its modern forms. No device or method, except abstension, is infallible. The most effective contraceptives are useless in the face of ignorance, carelessness or neglect. A pregnancy can impel the couple into a hasty, ill-considered marriage from which real depth of feeling is absent. Sometimes an abortion is sought as a desperate, last resort, but, as Jack Dominian states, 'Even those who believe abortion is morally legitimate must accept that to face a woman with the necessity for this action is neither responsible nor loving'. However, when all this has been said, the risk of pregnancy does not constitute on its own a sufficiently cogent basis for the Christian standard. Some men are infertile, some women cannot conceive, yet we would' expect the same standards of sexual morality from them as from others.

Fourth, statistics tend to show, according to the famous Kinsey Report (see also the next chapter), that a majority of those whose marriages end in divorce have had pre-marital sexual experience. People who have succeeded once in self-control (see Galatians 5:23 where self-control is described as a fruit of the Holy Spirit in one's life) are more likely to succeed again later and more likely to enjoy the unreserved confidence of their partner. Those who have accepted frustration with mature patience perhaps know better how to work for and accept satisfaction when it is eventually realised in a commitment made in marriage without reserve.

These four arguments against pre-marital sexual intercourse cannot be dismissed lightly, and cumulatively they have much force. But still they lack a certain cogency. Each can be got around by the exceptional case. How then can the strong doctrine advocated by Christians of 'no pre-marital sexual intercourse' be shown finally to be reasonable?

The answer lies in a true interpretation of what sexual intercourse within marriage means. Once this is understood, the unwisdom of intercourse in any other context becomes plainer. No one can deny that not all sex within marriage is ideal. It may mean 'I need satisfying' or 'I want pleasure'. Better, it may mean 'Let us enjoy each other'. Better still it may mean 'I love you and want to be closely united with you'. Sex is physical, but it is more than biological. Those who participate in it are persons and therefore have needs which operate on the deepest levels. When sex is enjoyed between a man and a woman who are mutually committed without reserve, each wanting the best for the other, each wanting their love to grow and deepen, each willing to stand by the other come what may, then the act is rich and overflowing with profoundly human significance for it symbolises all of these things, and more which cannot easily or adequately be put into words.

In sexual intercourse spouses say 'I am yours without reserve'. Outside marriage this cannot happen since fear of loss, jealousy, insecurity, exploitation all maintain too high a profile. In marriage these things are not always excluded, but the nature of a married commitment, properly undertaken, makes possible the reduction of such negative, destructive factors to a minimum. Married sex may mean 'Let us make a baby'. It means 'I am yours permanently'. It means 'Thank you for being you, for loving me, for being willing to share your whole life with me, for making me feel safe and complete'. It means 'We face the future optimistically together'. It means 'I'm sorry, let us be reconciled'. It means 'I am a man' or 'I am a woman'. It is, in Jack Dominian's phrase, 'a recurrent powerful source of sexual identification'.

If all this then is the true meaning of sexual intercourse in marriage, the same bodily act divorced from the 'without reserve' relationship only marriage allows will be shallow and superficial at best and downright evil at worst. To the extent that sexual intercourse is not accompanied by unreserved, mutual self-giving or is not an act of the whole person engaging body, mind, spirit and feelings, then to that extent it is a dehumanising act in which the actors are diminished as people.

69

Strong doctrine indeed! But we need to keep a true perspective. Is lust any worse than pride, a poisonous tongue or other less tangible sins? John 8:1-11 holds the answer. The reply of our Lord to the adulterous woman was a model of the elusive balance we seek in our ethics. He spoke strong words of mercy first: 'Neither do I condemn you.' Then came strong words of teaching and direction. 'Go, and do not sin again.' Strong mercy, strong doctrine.

12

Homosexuality

IN 1982 the Home Secretary in London announced to the world that Queen Elizabeth II's personal police officer had resigned because he had been involved in a homosexual relationship. There followed days of press articles and media discussion of the rights and wrongs of his resignation. Probably a majority of the self-appointed pundits concluded that the officer need not have resigned. Probably a majority of the public, claiming no expertise but giving vent to long-held instinctive attitudes, concluded that the palace was well rid of him. Amazingly, it was only in 1861 that the British substituted life imprisonment for the death penalty for a convicted sodomite (this word comes from the narrative concerning Sodom in Genesis 19 and sodomy means copulation between males or unnatural connection between human beings and animals). Back in 1290 the penalty in England for sodomy was burying alive!

Views about homosexuality, both in its male and female manifestations, have undergone change in recent years and even the Christian community finds within it a vocal minority urging a departure from the traditional stance that homosexual acts are sinful and require confession, repentance and forgiveness. It is probably true that 'the average Christian' (please forgive the phrase) holds views on homosexuality conditioned by the clear biblical statements on the subject. In short, he is against it. But now, such an attitude is under serious challenge from what have been regarded as respectable corners of the Christian community.

In the USA there is a whole new denomination of active homosexuals who profess to be evangelical and charismatic in their theology, the Metropolitan Community Church. It is said that its outreach has met with great response in the homosexual community. It is claimed by some that the Bible's statements have been misread. What are we to make of the witness of a man like H. A. Williams? He was a Fellow and Lecturer in Theology at

71

Trinity College, Cambridge, where he was also Dean of Chapel until 1969 when he became a member of the anglican religious order of the Community of the Resurrection at Mirfield in Yorkshire. He is widely regarded as a man of considerable spiritual insight and his writings are widely known. In his recent autobiography, *Some Day I'll Find You,* he tells of his homosexual experience. 'In my case homosexual feeling preceded puberty by a number of years. Among the questions I had to face *now I was beginning to be born anew, or raised from the dead,* was what to do about sex. I believe, and still believe, that it is always wrong to exploit people. But it became less and less obvious to me that sleeping with somebody, which for me meant another man, was necessarily in itself to exploit him. . . . I became more and more convinced that *if I was to achieve any sort of personal integrity I must have the courage to sleep with somebody.* During the next years I slept with several men, in each case fairly regularly.'

The italics in this quotation are mine. Williams' reputation is a high one in Christian circles. But he fails to show why being converted necessarily leads to sexual action. Not many converts have found such an impulse an immediate concomitant of serving Jesus. Secondly, he assumes that human appetites are for satisfying but that is not necessarily universally true. Thirdly, what would he have done had he been heterosexual? Would he have slept with 'several women'? Or what if he had seen some nexus between his conversion and coming to terms with material wealth? Would he have 'achieved integrity' by a series of 'several bank robberies'? Mr Williams account is honest but is it not one of the grossest rationalisations of error in modern Christian writing? Even the finest spirits, the finest minds, are subject to temptation and falling.

Society as a whole is in flux as regards sexual attitudes generally, and it comes as no surprise that codes of conduct cherished by many are being subjected to close re-examination. Voices are heard objecting to any suggestion that homosexuality is a 'perversion', although clearly it is so in the sense that it departs from the created order of sexuality designed to perpetuate the human species. Some decline to use the term 'perversion', preferring instead 'deviation' to indicate that no value-judgment is being made on the morality of the actions. Yet others, usually pro-homosexuality, regard it as merely a 'variant' on the broad spectrum of human sexuality. Whatever word is used, one thing is certain, that our language has been robbed for generations to come of the proper use of the word 'gay'.

Before proceeding further, an important distinction should be

72

drawn between the 'pervert' and the 'invert'. The pervert is basically heterosexual but has been drawn into homosexual practices by one circumstance or another, sometimes against his or her better judgment or sometimes as a willing partner in experimentation which becomes a habit. The invert, however, will probably never remember a time when the opposite sex was found sexually attractive. The inverted homosexual has never known a heterosexual orientation, but sometimes marriage is taken on in the hope of a 'cure'.

There can be no certainty about the causes of homosexual inversion, despite its widespread presence in many cultures, ages and civilisations. At best it may be said that its origins are found in a variety of factors: some inborn, some psychological, some physiological, some social. Modern research has concentrated on the possibility of inborn factors such as the effect of the male sex hormone, testosterone, on the central nervous system, and in turn upon adult sexual orientation. However, no conclusions have been reached. Upbringing and family circumstances have often been regarded as contributory, especially where the father is either weak or absent. In the end it is safest to say the causes are not known and that generalisations are out of place. Indeed, even about the appearance, personality and social grouping of homosexuals generalisations are misleading, although it is claimed that they readily recognise one another—by a glance, a movement or a certain pitch of voice.

How widespread is homosexuality in Western society? Major USA research carried out by Alfred Kinsey and published in 1948 *(Sexual Behaviour in the Human Male)* concluded that 4 per cent of the male population are exclusively homosexual, but that 5-10 per cent regard themselves as 'predominantly homosexual' with 25 per cent 'incidentally homosexual'. In 1965 Michael Schofield claimed that sexual experience whilst young does not always indicate sexual disposition in maturity *(Sociological Aspects of Homosexuality)*. He estimated that 44 per cent of non-homosexual men had homosexual experience before the age of 21 but did not develop these after that age. No figures are available on the incidence of lesbianism but Sidney Crown, a leading psychotherapist, has pointed out that homosexual women are more faithful in their relationships than homosexual men who tend to enter casual and frequent relationships.

The official salvationist approach to the matter is set out in *Positional Statements* (International Headquarters, 1980) where a distinction is drawn between homosexual acts on the one hand and, on the other, the orientation or sexual leaning which may or may not lead to such acts. The latter is deemed 'not blameworthy'. Our official view emphasises also the following: *(a)* a stable society requires stable family life; *(b)* both male and female homosexuality threaten family life; *(c)* the homosexual has to be understood and helped; *(d)* help is possible from various sources but pre-eminently from Jesus Christ who can liberate the whole person if there is submission to his will. This statement seeks the correct balance. It is compassionate without being over-indulgent; realistic about the sin involved without being homophobic. The statement searches for that elusive balance between strong doctrine and strong mercy. The need for balance was stressed by the American Christian writer, Dr Raymond Cox: 'The Church must not only maintain her biblically-based conviction about homosexuality . . . but must give equal—or even greater—emphasis to likewise biblically-based compassion for sinners whom God loves and wants to save and transform.' Cox asks if Jesus would have changed his 'Neither do I condemn thee: go, and sin no more' (John 8:11) if the woman taken in adultery had been a man taken in homosexuality. Clearly not.

The same balance is not always evident in Christian attitudes today and has not been consistently present in the past. Augustine, in his *Confessions,* refers to Genesis 19 and to 'shameful acts against nature . . . to be detested and punished'. Thomas Aquinas regarded homosexual acts as the most serious of all sins of lust apart from bestiality. Martin Luther regarded sodomy as idol worship and John Calvin called it 'the fearful crime of unnatural lust'. More recently, Karl Barth *(Church Dogmatics)* has written of 'a masculinity free from women' which leads to 'corrupt emotional and finally physical desire . . . a sexual union which is not and cannot be genuine'. Helmut Thielicke *(The Ethics of Sex)* thinks Barth too harsh, and urges for the Church a new degree of pastoral sympathy, especially for the homosexually biased person who has not arrived at his condition through dissolute experimentation. Thielicke's view is that heterosexual sinners have no superior vantage point from which to look down on homosexual sinners.

Several helpful statements have emerged in recent years which match the Army's search for a balance between sound teaching for the flock and sound compassion for the homosexual, whether or not he is part of that flock, the people of God. The Catholic Social Welfare Commission, in *An Introduction to the Pastoral Care of Homosexual People,* draws a line between homosexual orientation and homosexual practice. 'Homosexuality (or homophilia) as such is neither morally good nor bad. Homosexuality, like hetero-sexuality, is a state or condition. It is morally neutral and the invert homosexual, like the heterosexual, cannot be held responsible for his tendencies. . . . With regard to homosexual acts, Scripture and the on-going tradition of Christianity make it quite clear that those are immoral. Whatever pastoral judgment may conclude concerning personal responsibility in a particular case, it is clear that in the objective order homosexual acts may not be approved.' The document goes on to reassert that sexual intercourse is proper only to the holy estate of matrimony. But the entire second half of the statement sets out, sensitively, pastoral guidelines for those helping homosexuals to understand and examine the meaning of their conduct in the light of the love of God and the love of neighbour.

These pastoral guidelines are drawn upon substantially by the Church of Scotland in their 1982 statement on homosexuality. The sinfulness of homosexual conduct is stated clearly but the response of the church is said to be 'that of one pilgrim humbly seeking to share the burden of another on the journey through life, in pursuit of God's will'. Great emphasis is placed on seeking first a true understanding of homosexuality and then on sharing one's experience of new life and new power in Jesus, which 'does not mean instant serenity'.

Very recently, Christian documents have appeared in the UK as elsewhere, promoting a view of homosexuality very far from the Army's. In 1979 the Family Life Committee of the Methodist Conference published *A Christian Understanding of Human Sexuality*. The bulk of the paper spells out the following:

1 No persons can be held responsible for their orientation, but they are responsible for the way they act.
2 Sexuality cannot be categorised so as totally to distinguish one person from another. Rather, homosexuality should be seen as a point on a continuous spectrum of human sexuality.
3 A pre-eminent place is given to Scripture, but precise moral guidance cannot easily be extracted directly from that source.
4 The Christian idea of love is one in which the beloved finds fulfilment. Exploitation is excluded.
5 If sexuality is physically expressed, the goodness or badness of the choice as to how it is expressed can be assessed only by the quality of love appropriate to a particular relationship.
6 Personal relationships are a basic part of being human, and forming stable relationships may be an appropriate way of expressing a homosexual orientation.
7 The morality of any such physical expression is to be assessed by the same criteria which are applied to heterosexual relationships.
8 The only ultimate scandal is lovelessness.

Readers will understand the outcry raised in methodist circles by this statement. Although it was not adopted at a later Methodist Conference (June 1982) it is significant that it was produced at all. A fairly similar view is hinted at in *God's Yes to Sexuality* (1981) produced by a working party appointed by the British Council of Churches. Even the Roman catholic community spawns dissenters. A committee of the Catholic Theological Society of America stated in 1977, contrary to the teaching of their church, that 'homosexuals have the same right to love, intimacy, and relationships as heterosexuals'.

All the liberal statements hinge upon a liberal view of the scriptural references to homosexual conduct. Indeed, the methodist document thinks there might be no 'biblical view', and that the texts seen as binding can be dismissed as limited to their own day, outmoded by 'modern knowledge', or typical of 'Paul's Jewishness'. No mention is made that Paul's Jewishness was the seed-bed God picked out for the initial growth and consolidation of Christian thinking in its infancy.

It is a highly dangerous technique for Christians to write off the Bible in forming a Christian moral stance on any topic of current concern. It is not enough to say that 'modern knowledge' has rendered God's eternal word irrelevant. At the deepest level we have no further knowledge of homosexuality today than thousands of years ago. Even if we had, the Scriptures are very plain indeed on the subject and we depart from them at our peril.

There are five passages which directly teach that homosexual behaviour is contrary to the will of God. Leviticus 18:22 and 20:13 are unambiguous. That they are part of the Hebrew law codes does not diminish their value today any more than the value of the Ten Commandments is diminished. Romans 1:26, 27 prohibits both male and female homosexual acts. This is not merely a condemnation of sexual experimentation, for in the context of Romans 1-3, Paul addresses the more general question of the unreason and unnaturalness which are the consequence of turning from God. Homosexuality is thus regarded as contrary to the law of nature, that is, human nature as God intended it. In 1 Corinthians 6:9, 10, we read that unrepentant homosexuals living out their chosen lifestyle without efforts to control or reorient their appetites do not belong to the Kingdom of God. The verses do not, as has been argued, refer only to homosexual prostitutes. Finally, 1 Timothy 1:8-10 endorses the earlier pronouncements.

There are, in addition, passages which imply the sinfulness of homosexual acts. Those are Genesis 19:4-9; Judges 19:22-26; 2 Peter 2:1-22 and Jude 3-23. The story of Sodom in Genesis 19 has been much discussed in homophile literature. It is argued that the sin there was not homosexuality but homosexual rape and that inhospitability is the main sin condemned. However, a Hebrew reader, knowing of Leviticus, would most certainly see the homosexual acts as depraved and the force as an aggravation of that depravity.

Debate in Christian circles has raised the question of whether the biblical pronouncements, particularly those in the New Testament, apply equally to homosexual acts by both the pervert and invert homosexual. It is clear that the conduct of the pervert is not approved. But what of the invert whose orientation has never been other than it is? David Field addresses this issue in his splendid book, *The Homosexual Way* (IVP, 1979). He considers the terms used by Paul when writing about homosexuality: 'The most common word, *arsenokoites,* covers all homosexual behaviour. It is made up of the words for 'male' and 'sexual intercourse' and simply describes the act of homosexual union without any hint of discrimination between inverts or perverts or between loving and casual sex. Paul could have chosen more specific terms such as *paiderastes* ('lover of boys') or *paidophthoros* ('corrupter of boys') or *arrenomanes* ('mad after males'). But he went for the most general word available.

This is confirmed by a true understanding of what Paul is saying in Romans 1 (see above). The general context is that of the creation. In verse 26 the phrase 'natural relations' is used. These were given up in exchange for 'unnatural', by both men and women. It is an unjustified interpretation of the passage to claim that it exempts the invert from censure since his only 'natural' relations are with those of his own sex. Rather, Paul is talking about 'natural relations' between human beings as created by God, that is, natural in terms of heterosexual activity designed to perpetuate the human race created by God. The 'exchange' is that of natural heterosexual conduct generally for unnatural homosexual conduct generally. The question of invert or pervert is simply not addressed. Both fall within the concept of 'unnatural'.

In concluding, we should remind ourselves again of the Army's statement 'that we should seek, in the spirit of Jesus Christ, to understand and help the homosexual'. It seems few seek psychiatric treatment in an effort to change their sexual orientation. Of those who do, few become exclusively heterosexual, but of those initially bisexual, about 50 per cent become non-homosexual in practice. The concept of a 'cure' may be misplaced in dealing with this very real human problem. Almost all those Christians actively engaged in seeking to counsel homosexuals would agree that it is at best naïve and at worst extremely hurtful to assume that a person will

77

suddenly switch from one sexual orientation to another. That is why Christian counsel will aim to encourage the homosexual person in a self-disciplined, celibate life-style, parallel to that of the unmarried heterosexual person.

The resources of the gospel add immeasurably to the likelihood of success. Assuming that by 'cure' Henry Drummond meant the limited aim just mentioned, we note with interest his statement in *The Ideal Life*: 'Christianity professes to cure anything. The process may be slow, the discipline may be severe, but it can be done. But is it not a constitutional thing . . . and can *that* be cured? Yes, if there is anything in Christianity. If there is no provision for that, then Christianity stands convicted of being unequal to human need.'

13
Pornography

FIRST, we must define our terms. The word 'pornography' stems from two Greek words which in turn mean 'harlot' (or 'prostitute') and 'writing'. So, strictly, pornography is any written material which has for its subject anything related to the activities of prostitutes. By extension it has come to mean any written matter which deals with any sexual activity in such a way that accepted standards in society are offended. In particular, the writer of pornography refers to sex in a very overt and unsubtle way. He allows his work to become impermissibly erotic in a deliberate attempt to arouse the sexual feelings of the reader. This is done by words or pictures or both.

Commonly mentioned alongside pornography is the word 'obscenity'. It is a mistake to equate the two. This word derives from the Latin word for 'filth' and should properly be used with reference to that which is unconnected with sex but which nevertheless outrages or offends commonly accepted standards in society. For instance, a writer or artist may make explicit reference to the excretory functions of the body. If this is too explicit, it constitutes obscenity even though sex is not involved. Similarly with the theme of violence. If it, too, is treated in an over-explicit fashion, again obscenity is the result. This chapter will deal mainly with pornography as over against obscenity.

Our topic is far from straightforward and there are no easy solutions. We could quite naïvely call for the suppression by force if need be of all written or pictorial material dealing with sex. But what then of school textbooks? What then of genuinely helpful articles in women's magazines aimed at dispelling the myths and old wives' tales that surround the subject? What also of artistic freedom and of literary merit in works which treat seriously sexual relations between men and women but may nevertheless offend some folk? Where is the line to be drawn?

Can we talk absolutes in this complex and troublesome area of morals?

It seems not. Some sort of balance must be struck. High-handed censorship will work injustice and bring unreasonable results in cases such as those mentioned above. On the other hand, total freedom of expression, or licence, will expose the vulnerable to much that is undesirable and indeed positively harmful. There has to be a middle way, but we shall return to this later.

There are many and varied interests to be taken into account: the press and newspapers, radio and television, book publications, the cinema, public libraries and so on. All have a stake in the censor-ship debate but so, too, has the public at large. Perhaps the paramount interest is that of the young and the innocent, not forgetting those who are psychologically vulnerable to the adverse effects of pornographic literature. Balancing fairly all these interests is well-nigh impossible. If we err, it should be on the side of protection. But what is the law to do? Outright prohibitions seldom work and so English law, for example, has attempted to control pornography and obscenity as follows.

Back in 1868 Chief Justice Cockburn handed down a judgment which stood for decades as the ruling precedent. He said that the material produced stood in breach of the law if it tended *to deprave and corrupt* those whose minds are open to such immoral influences and into whose hands a publication of the sort in question might fall. The words in italics are the crucial ones. Regrettably they are notoriously difficult to define and many a lawyer has earned a fat fee arguing their meaning before the judges.

The difficulty of applying Cockburn CJ's ruling to any given case is at once apparent. What if I write a serious textbook on human biology intending it for adults only and yet it falls by accident into the hands of a child? On the 1868 decision I am to be convicted. For reasons like this and others, England introduced in 1959 the Obscene Publications Act. This removes the risk for a writer who writes with integrity for adults but whose work falls by chance into the hands of minors. Further, the work is to be assessed on its merits as a whole, not just by one or two passages, and there can be no conviction in the criminal courts if the publication in question is justified as being for the public good on the grounds that it is in the interests of science, literature, art or learning, or of other objects of general concern. The Act also insists that the court should listen to the evidence of expert witnesses who will be able to speak about the artistic worth of the work.

It should perhaps be said that such witnesses can always be found for either or any point of view and so the value of their testimony is limited. English law has still not found the answer. In America the same problems have been met. There the legal test for obscenity was to ask if the material held 'an appeal to prurience' and suffered from 'an utter lack of social significance', but again these phrases defy definition and the results were less than satisfactory. The search for proper and effective legislation still goes on.

Such legislation should it seems reflect the views of the society it aims to protect, but how are those views to be determined? Your view and mine may or may not be poles apart. And in any case, should the law of the land reflect the attitudes of one section of the community more than those of another? Should the law reflect Christian values even when the majority are not Christians? There is a good case for saying yes to this. Society works best when its moral standards are highest. It remains in the interests of the many that Christians should impress upon the authorities their particular slant on things and then, if legislation is to be drafted, to bring pressure to bear so that it is at the very least not inconsistent with Christian thinking.

What then is Christian thinking on pornography? Even here we meet a variety of views and so these following remarks must necessarily be general. We who follow Jesus claim that there are certain moral laws which never change. Human perception of those laws may change but the laws themselves stand inviolate through the ages. They have to do with integrity and purity and they have been laid down once and for all by God. 'Whatever is true, honourable, just, pure, lovely, gracious, if there is any excellence, if there is anything worthy of praise, think about these things' (Philippians 2:4). 'Immorality and all impurity . . . must not even be named among you, as is fitting among saints. Let there be no filthiness, nor silly talk, nor levity which are not fitting. . . . Be sure of this, that no immoral or impure man . . . has any inheritance in the kingdom of Christ and of God' (Ephesians 5:3-5). 'Do you not know that you are God's temple and that God's spirit dwells in you? . . . For God's temple is holy, and that temple you are' (1 Corinthians 3:16, 17). 'You have learned that they were told, "Do not commit adultery." But what I tell you is this: "If a man looks on a woman with a lustful eye, he has already committed adultery with her in his heart"' (Matthew 5:27, 28). Such Bible teaching must be the cornerstone of any Christian approach to the pornography issue. It is strong teaching, strong doctrine.

Christian attitudes will spring from Christian views on human sexuality. We oppose pornography not because we think sex is objectionable—far from it—but because sex is sacred and ought not to be degraded. In 1976 the Roman catholic Archbishop of

Toronto published this statement in an open letter: 'It is through our God-given sexuality that we as human beings can reach out to one another in love. It is in sexual union that a couple can express to one another tenderness, intimacy and permanent fidelity. The public and profitable exploitation of the sexual, so common around us, is *a direct betrayal of the basic value of sexuality itself.* What is sometimes referred to as "the playboy philosophy" of sexuality, using and discarding another person with "no strings attached", is not a form of freedom but enslavement. What was intended to be most precious becomes trivial. What was created to be most deeply personal is dehumanised.'

In 1972 Lord Longford published a report on pornography in Britain. Extracts from this report might help to show the diseased nature of our society and the utterly dreadful consequences pornography addiction might bring:

We offer a few selected cases—not as evidence medical or otherwise, but as examples that may help the reader to appreciate the kind of problems which make certain individuals peculiarly vulnerable to the effects we believe commercial pornographers are likely to exploit. Two doctors wrote to us to describe a 17-year-old patient of theirs who, thanks to great exertions by the Mental Welfare Officer, his employers, his priest and the doctors themselves, was helped to retain his hold on sanity, albeit tenuously. The young man recently went quite legally to a cinema in a neighbouring town advertising sex films. He returned, rushed round his home in a frenzied state and then went out and sexually assaulted a girl of five. . . .

We received the following letter from a 15-year-old schoolboy:
'Dear Lord Longford, the most important thing about pornography is that it does literally corrupt. In all boys' schools pornography plays an important part of the average boy's life. In the boarding school here the effect is very noticeable. The fact is that pornography does not satisfy, but rather builds up people's emotions. . . . There is a lending "library" of sex magazines in the boarding house which consists of the dirtiest magazines available. Pornography is like a disease; it starts with mild forms of magazines like *Playboy* in our second and third years and ends up in our fourth and fifth years with pictures of lesbians, descriptions of sodomy, etc. The result in our class is a crowd of people who want sex in any form.'

The next incident is not, we believe, by any means unique. It is one where a youth died because of the exploitation of the permissive society. The facts are these. A young boy, successful at school and at sport, was found hanging with a copy of a popular paper open in front of him. The pathologist described the incident as a 'sex experiment' and attacked the editor of the paper for publishing an article on the subject. 'The unfortunate youth,' said the pathologist, 'had been motivated by the erotic pictures of half-naked girls and particularly of one with a rope pulled round her neck.' He added: 'In practically every case of this kind which it is my unfortunate duty to investigate there is pornographic literature lying about.'

It has been argued that evidence from Denmark shows that the rate of sex-linked crime drops when laws against pornography are relaxed. Under Danish law pornography was legalised in 1969. It is true that statistics for sexual offences have gone down since that date. But what the humanists do not reveal is that other changes in the law at about the same time can account for the lower statistics: 11 categories of crime were removed from the statute book; the upper age limit for a minor was reduced from 17 to 13 years. No wonder the statistics are different! In any case, the number of rapes in Denmark in the same period rose significantly: 173 in 1963, 280 in 1977, and 484 in 1978.

In his invaluable, expert study of this subject, John H. Court (*Pornography: A Christian Critique,* IVP, 1980) states: 'Where pornography has become available, serious sex offences have gone steeply upward in frequency.' He cites statistics from Los Angeles where sex offences rose by 56 per cent between 1958 and 1973. In England and Wales police figures show a steady increase in reported sex crimes from 30.7 per 100,000 population in 1950 to 49.6 in 1970—an increase of 62 per cent. The incidence of the offence of having intercourse with a girl under 13 years of age rose by 44 per cent between 1963 and 1973; over the same period, reports of rape were up by 183 per cent and other offences against females were up by 60 per cent.

John H. Court has carried out studies of sexual offence statistics on a comparative basis between those countries giving greater freedom to pornography and those with more restrictive laws. The following is the percentage increase in the number of reported rapes in the 'freer' countries since 1964:

USA	139 per cent
England and Wales	94 per cent
Australia	160 per cent
New Zealand	107 per cent
Copenhagen	84 per cent

The rate of increase is significantly lower in countries continuing restraint:

Singapore	69 per cent
South Africa	28 per cent

In Japan, where an even more restrictive policy is pursued, a decrease of 49 per cent in reported rapes has been registered since 1964. These figures do not prove conclusively a causal link between pornography and sex offences, but they are good reason for a major re-examination of the issue by governments.

Some will disagree and claim that there are no fixed entities such as obscenity and pornography and there is no proof that exposure to them (if they exist) in fact depraves. This is the liberal (or perhaps better the libertarian) view which is heard from those who see themselves as unshockable. They are far too sophisticated for that! Their case finds support in the absence of any truly scientific data on the role of pornography in human sexual response. On the other hand, it has often been suggested that the viewing of excessively violent or sexually explicit scenes in a movie can produce in us even a slightly more cruel or sexually orientated attitude to those around us.

Further, pornography works by hallucination. It is a cheat. The reader or watcher is intended to be sexually aroused as if he were actually experiencing the things of which he is reading or viewing. Therefore the ultimate it can bring is disappointment. It is artificial and vicarious sexual enjoyment, sex out of context, and thereby finally adds only to the frustration and dissatisfaction of the one indulging in it.

Young people who are exposed to this sort of material are in danger of being (to use one writer's phrase) 'precociously excited into sexuality' with the attendant risks of acquiring an artificial and distorted idea of what should rightly be a fine and lovely part of human life. Sex is essentially an expression of one's deepest feelings for another person. Seen in this light it is highly personal and very private. To expose the sexual activities of others to general view is to deny the privacy inherent in sex.

Perhaps once upon a time our primitive ancestors copulated in full view of others. But with the advance of civilisation we have carefully constructed inhibitions and sublimations with regard to sexuality and violence which now form the very foundations of our communal existence. Hence humans today seek privacy for their sexual activity. Pornography reverses this trend and is an attempt, in the name of making money, to dehumanise and re-primitivise man.

The book shops abound today in soft and not so soft pornography and it seems that the public will buy all it can get its hands on. The sexual subtones and the overtly sexual passages purposely designed to titillate the reader are pounced on eagerly. The book is bought and the creator of the damage thereby enriched and encouraged to still greater efforts to produce more of the same. He knows that if he sprinkles blasphemies and obscenities throughout his work he will make money. All the while he fools himself that he is emancipated. What he fails to realise is that he differs only in age from the tiny tot who giggles at his own great daring in making a joke about the toilet! Why should we allow the graffiti of childhood to persist into our adult lives? Why should we permit the regressive, backward-looking elements in our make-up to win control when it comes to coping with sexual stress?

Donald Soper links the rise in pornography with the increase in the leisure time we have since automation in the world of industry. He says that the more time a man has on his hands to idle away, the more likely it is that his mind will come to dwell upon that which is unwholesome. Hence the Bible's injunction to think upon that which is pure and lovely and of good report. Simple prohibition is not enough. There is a need to be occupied with creative work so that all the personality is employed. In particular, the regressed side of the personality needs work to do, but it must be something worth doing. Sometimes only formal psychotherapy will achieve this, but usually all it takes is a less formal and non-sexual sublimating activity.

Expert help may be required by those becoming addicted to pornography. In some users there develops a psychological dependency on pornographic materials. I have met only two men who were addicts. Both were wretched in their self-disgust. The Christian, in such an encounter, remembers his strong doctrine, but he prays for strong mercy and true insight. One man was ridden with guilt, enslaved. His home was piled high with books, magazines and erotica. The road to recovery started when confession was blurted out and the rich help and grace of God invoked. He returned home, gathered up every 'obscene book or paper' (the phrase used in The Salvation Army's articles of war, signed by every soldier of the Army) he had accumulated, piled it before him and then knelt in prayer: 'Lord Jesus, here are my magazines. They are filthy and abhorrent to me, yet they bind both my body and my soul. You take them, please. You will know what to do with them. I want no more of them. Thank you, Lord. Amen.' Then he burned them all. Daily after that the struggle raged in him. The last time I saw him he was still victorious, daily temptation being overcome daily in Christ. I cannot report that the second man defeated his addiction. Faith, for him, was hard.

David Field and Peter Toon (*Life Questions,* Lion Publishing, 1982) quote a doctor who was a pornography addict: 'For about 10 years I had been hooked on pornographic magazines which I

bought and kept locked away in a cupboard. . . . For years I had
been trying to throw these papers away but couldn't bring myself to
do it. . . . Addiction to pornography is like a cancer of the mind.'
Christians believe that sex is good in itself. We also believe that
the naked human body is good in itself. What we oppose is the
abuse of these lovely things in the name of art or in the name of
making a fast profit. No one who follows Jesus condemns sex.
Rather it is undesirable sexual practices that we oppose. It is the
cheapening of sex that makes us angry, when that which is meant
by God to lead to joy and beauty leads only to cheap sniggers and,
via artificiality, to deep disappointment. No Christian will deny the
importance of sex in human life, but as a child of God he will seek
God's purpose with regard to his sexual impulses. Why has this
potent and explosive force been given to us? What are we to make
of it? The person who honestly faces these questions in the light of
the teaching of Jesus will soon see the incompatibility of both
following Jesus and seeking to enjoy pornographic material.
John H. Court summarises the Christian response to pornography in 12 short statements. It is:

1   anti-life (it is destructive)
2   anti-family (it ridicules marriage)
3   anti-human (it is animalistic)
4   anti-woman (it degrades women)
5   anti-children (it abuses children)
6   anti-sex (it debases sex and undermines the user's potential for
    satisfying relationships)
7   anti-social (it triggers crime)
8   anti-environment (it pollutes streets and shops)
9   anti-community (it panders to human weakness)
10 anti-culture (it fails to ennoble or enrich)
11 anti-conscience (it hardens responses to sexual and violent
    exploitation)
12 anti-God (it is opposed to the teachings of the Bible about purity
    and love)

If we are to do anything at all about the rising sales of
pornography, what should it be? Legal prohibitions do not work or
at best they work injustice as we have seen. Yet the law has to play a
role of some sort. Only the law can provide effective protection for
the young, weak or vulnerable amongst us. Outright bans on the
one hand and total licence on the other are not the answer. The
middle way is that of control and regulation.
There are methods of ensuring that a rough balance be struck
between freedom of expression and protection of the weak or

86

immature. We look to those in authority to regulate the flow of this material so that such persons come to no harm. For example, we expect fair warning of television shows which might be damaging, we expect high standards of moral integrity from book and newspaper publishers and from film makers. Moreover we expect their respective professional bodies to act responsibly in this field and to impose sanctions and disciplinary measures where the professional codes are breached. Where need be the codes themselves must be revised to heighten their moral content.

Further, we expect our local shopkeeper to empty his shop of all pornographic material whether hard or soft. Perhaps this is the best way for the individual Christian to be effective. What is to stop us from politely informing any shop proprietor we have dealings with that until he withdraws from public view and from his stocks all offensive publications we shall withdraw our custom and shall actively but privately encourage others to do the same? Hit in his pocket, he will respond.

At the same time we will go on searching for a truly scriptural insight into the nature of human sexuality. We will teach our children accordingly and counsel our teenagers, courting couples and married couples that sex has profound emotional and spiritual implications as important as and intertwined with the physical. More and more we will learn the art of educating our own people, but also public opinion, so that the worthless is rejected in preference to the wholesome.

Perhaps the last word should go to D. H. Lawrence, much maligned and much misunderstood novelist: 'Even I would censor pornography rigorously. It would not be very difficult. In the first place, genuine pornography is almost always underworld, it doesn't come into the open. In the second, you can recognise it by the insult it offers, invariably, to sex and to the human spirit.'

14

Punishment and forgiveness

THE chances are that every reader of this chapter has at some time or other imposed a punishment upon another person. It is even more likely that every reader has been the recipient of a punishment. The subject is no mere academic one. It plays an important role in schools; perhaps an even more important one in the home; and in society generally the principles of justice upon which all of us rely are enforced by means of punishments handed down in the courts. Personalities can be made or marred by the types of punishment received, their frequency, their manner of infliction and the time period involved.

Capital punishment has been abandoned in many western countries in the last 20 years. In 1983 the British parliament rejected its restoration after fierce public debate. Underlying the issue is the question of whether it is moral to punish at all.

So why punish? What are the theories behind the infliction of punishment? By what right do we punish? Is punishment consistent with Christian teaching? Where does the concept of forgiveness come into it? This chapter will try to answer at least some of these questions, but note that we are in an area of debate where there is room for more than one point of view.

It should help as a start to say what we mean by punishment. One famous lawyer from the past, Hugo Grotius, defined it as 'the infliction of an ill suffered for an ill done'. In more recent times Professor H. L. A. Hart, an English legal philosopher, has expanded this definition to indicate the following five ingredients of any action claiming to constitute a punishment:

1 It must be unpleasant.

2 A rule or rules, either formal or informal, must have been breached.
3 It must be inflicted upon an alleged offender for his offence.
4 It must be intentionally administered by humans.
5 It must be imposed by the authority against whom the offence was committed.

Clearly, Hart's definition can apply equally to a formal courtroom situation and to the less formal setting of the home or the school.

Is it morally right to punish? We would all reply at once that it is, but then how can we go on to demonstrate the rightness of it? We might feel it to be right, but we have also to be able to explain why it is right. There seem to be three main ways of justifying a punishment: *(a)* to say it is deserved (the *retribution* theory); *(b)* to say it will deter (the *deterrence* theory); *(c)* to say it will reform the offender (the *reform* theory).

Looking in turn at these approaches, it will be seen that the retribution theory is not a fashionable one. The other two enjoy much greater popularity, but then fashion and truth are not always identical. Even the gospel is unfashionable, but that fact alone cannot invalidate it.

The retribution theory of punishment (not, incidentally, to be confused with notions of revenge or blood feud) states that a punishment is morally justified only if it is deserved, that is to say, only if it bears a reasonable proportion to the offence committed. There has to be a correspondence between the gravity of the offence and the severity of the punishment. This is a vital ingredient of meeting the demands of justice. The theory says that he who causes pain must in turn be made to suffer pain. The punishment is given, not despite the fact that it hurts, but precisely because it hurts. Justice is achieved by ensuring that the guilty offender suffers discomfort of some kind, but, above all, that discomfort must bear a reasonable relation to the gravity of the offence committed.

Supporters of the deterrence and reform theories regard all punishment as inherently evil. They are prepared, however, to tolerate it if it will achieve some recognised goal beyond itself, for instance, deterrence or reform.

The deterrence theory sees the justification for punishment in the fact (or supposed fact) that it will deter others from committing the same offence. This view allows for an increase in the suffering of the offender on the grounds that there will be a corresponding increase in the general happiness of society, where, theoretically,

89

there will be less crime due to potential offenders having been deterred. In this sense the interests of the individual criminal are subordinated to the wider interests of society.

Also seeking a goal beyond mere punishment, the reform theory sees the penalty as morally justified only if it will reform or cure the offender of his criminal tendencies. So here the punishment is seen as moral medicine. It may be unpleasant, but it is surely wholesome!

We can try to assess the merits of these three very different points of view. Taking the reform theory first, it has to be said that it has never satisfactorily been shown that inflicting pain has a causal connection with an inner change in a man's moral behaviour and standards. So whilst the aim of reforming a man is a worthy one, it remains doubtful whether this can be achieved in a penal setting. Apart from this there are very clear dangers to be recognised in this approach. Its advocates speak of 'treating' a man for his waywardness instead of 'punishing' him. This sounds fine and humanitarian, even compassionate, but a moment's thought will suffice to show that the so-called 'treatment' is not voluntarily undertaken by the offender and is in fact every bit as compulsory as a punishment in the normal sense.

Then there is the question of how long the 'treatment' is to last. The reform theorists reply that it will last as long as it takes to cure the man. But what about his just deserts? Can we claim it is morally right to 'treat' a shoplifter for, say, 15 years, just because that is how long he may take to be reformed, when normally he would receive a much lighter penalty? To ask only 'Will it cure?' is not good enough. We must also ask, as a first consideration, 'Is it fair?' and 'Does he deserve it?'

So, we arrive back at the retribution theory and it begins to look, despite its off-putting name, as if it might offer stronger mercy in the end than the theory of reform!

One more word on this: if we are going to justify punishment on the basis of cure alone, then we would be giving ourselves the moral right to take those who have in fact committed no offence at all but who are deemed by psychiatrists and the like to be highly probable future offenders and to subject them compulsorily to 'treatment'. Echoes of totalitarianism! It should be unnecessary to elaborate on the scope for abuse inherent in such a system. When we see signs that the state penal system no longer demands a clear and visible link between punishment and guilt, that is the time to beware and the time to make our voices heard.

Coming now to the deterrent theory, we should note that it too has serious weaknesses. Obviously the idea of deterring potential offenders is a good one, but a deterrent effect cannot be measured, for by its very nature it produces an absence of results. To make it the sole criterion for imposing punishment is questionable for, like the reform theory, it neglects the question of the offender's just deserts. In considering the morality of a punishment, this theory asks only, 'Will it deter others?'. The prior point of whether it is fair and just for the one punished need never come into the picture. So we would thereby have a right to hang, draw and quarter all who drop litter in public places since this might well have a deterrent effect upon the other members of society not inclined to the use of public litter bins! Further, to deter effectively, it is not logically necessary to prove first the accused man's guilt. The deterrent will operate well merely if the public think he is guilty, thus opening wide the door to what the press calls 'show trials'. This approach would permit us to deter some by unjustifiably punishing others, including those normally excused by the law—the insane, the infant or the automaton who cannot help his actions.

So we must reiterate that no punishment is morally acceptable unless it is securely tied into a finding of guilt in the one to be punished. Only if it is fair to him can we then ask if what we are doing will also, but incidentally, deter others or have a reformative effect upon the offender. This brings us back squarely yet again to the retribution theory. It is potentially the most merciful approach of all for it places at the top of the priority list the question: 'Is this punishment fair and just in the sense that it follows a clear finding of guilt and is in proportion to the gravity of the offence committed?' It ensures categorically, unlike the other two theories, that before a penalty is inflicted the recipient has been found guilty. A fundamental principle of justice requires that a man should not be punished more severely than he deserves. C. S. Lewis claims that the retribution theory safeguards this principle as no other does: 'I urge a return to the retributive theory not only or even primarily in the interest of society, but in the interests of the criminal.'

The theory also ensures freedom from punishment for the innocent. As we have seen above, the other theories, as a matter of logical necessity, cannot offer the same guarantee. In this sense the retribution theory limits the area of morally acceptable punishments. Furthermore, if the innocent are not to be punished, it would seem that a morally acceptable penal system should provide for the possibility of reparation in the event of a miscarriage of justice coming to light. This would be reason enough for granting no place in a penal system to the obviously irrevocable death penalty.

If the best justification for punishing is retribution, this is not to deny altogether a role to the reform and deterrent aspects. Although we accept justice as the first and foremost concern, provided that that is adequately safeguarded, there is then every reason to consider the effects of any given penalty upon the rest of society and upon the offender's own future conduct. Justice first, deterrence and reform second.

Where does the idea of Christian forgiveness come in? If an offender is to be restored, can he be both punished and forgiven? Are the two compatible? Is it possible to forgive and thereafter punish without negating the forgiveness? Norman H. Snaith, the distinguished Old Testament scholar, writing about the scriptural concept of forgiveness (*The Book of Job*, SCM, 1968), says that it 'covers' the sin 'so that it no longer obtrudes between man and God' and leaves 'no resentment or anger in the mind of the injured party'. The New Testament requires the follower of Jesus to imitate his Lord in this very matter of forgiving. (See Matthew 5:48 for the general point and then Ephesians 4:32 and Colossians 3:13).

We who preach the gospel of salvation do so because we believe it is possible for sinners to be restored to a right relationship with their Maker. This restoration is not the mere outward conforming of behaviour hoped for by advocates of the reform theory. Behavioural reform is not the same as inner renewal and spiritual restoration, for it seems that this latter can be achieved only if forgiveness is offered to the offender—forgiveness by the victim of the offence and by the rest of us too as shown by the way the offender is treated upon his return to society, the degree to which he is accepted by us, and the ease with which he is given work, shelter and support following release.

But what about the punishment if the offender is forgiven? Certainly it is possible both to punish and forgive, even to forgive and then punish. This is the case with a parent admonishing his child or a teacher his pupil. How this works in the context of the state punishing a criminal is less clear, but the considerations mentioned at the end of the last paragraph are relevant. Moreover, being slow to forgive jeopardises our own right to receive forgiveness. Mark 11:25 quotes Jesus as saying, 'Whenever you stand praying, forgive, if you have anything against anyone; so that your Father also who is in heaven may forgive you your trespasses' *(RSV)*. The parable of the unforgiving servant makes the same point in Matthew 18:23-25. From this it is only a short step to the conclusion that a willingness to forgive is in fact not only the precondition of ourselves being forgiven but the precondition of having any right to punish at all.

If we refuse to forgive, then we punish without the moral right to punish. Not only this, but the punishment will fail in any attempt to restore the offender as a total person—body, mind and soul. The weak alternative is to settle for merely reforming his outward conduct by subjecting him to 'treatment'. It is forgiveness alone which heals and restores.

15

'Salvationist' ethics?

'IN the past it did not seem necessary to supply grounds for salvationist religious or moral and social attitudes. Now, when respect for biblical authority is less widely felt and the old time morals more generally questioned, some defining of Salvation Army principles and explanation of our stand where they may seem controversial should be helpful.' Thus said Bernard Watson in introducing his splendid account of Army attitudes on social and moral issues, *The Salvationist in a Secular Society* (Salvationist Publishing and Supplies, Ltd, 1974).

The passing of another decade has done nothing to diminish the need for 'explanation' and this book is an attempt to aid the process. However, some will ask whether the Army has anything distinctive to contribute to Christian ethics generally. Does it make sense to speak of 'salvationist ethics'? It certainly makes literal sense. Salvationist ethics means quite simply salvationist conduct or standards of behaviour. But we need to note a distinction before going on. There are standards prescribed for salvationists, standards to which soldiers of the Army are expected to adhere. Then there is conduct which salvationists would be happy to see followed even by those not in the Army. This book has tended to equate the two, for no salvationist would advocate a standard for a non-salvationist without being willing to keep it himself. On the other hand, our own standards can never be arbitrarily imposed on others; we might advise, counsel, even preach a given ethical position, but there is a line beyond which it would be quite wrong to go. The line is crossed when counsel to the non-salvationist becomes insistence. With our own people, insistence has its place and where the standard is found too arduous (I do not say 'too high' for that is to claim superiority) a change in the person's relationship to the Army may have to ensue.

One reason for not 'insisting' with regard to ethics, quite apart

94

from the impracticality of such an approach is that salvationist ethics are theological ethics, with roots deep in beliefs about God. Unless the beliefs are shared, the ethics cannot be. Hubert R. Scotney, in his article, 'Salvationist Ethics in a Secularist Society' (*The Officer,* January 1980) reminds us that in the articles of war, signed by every salvation soldier, we find the ethical demands in the second half of the document flowing naturally from the earlier statements of religious doctrine. He says: 'Because we hold certain convictions therefore we pledge ourselves to act in particular ways. Dogma is immediately translated into ethics.'

This is true of all Christian ethics and salvationist ethics are Christian ethics. They are rooted in dogma, but it is Christian dogma. For this reason salvationist ethics rely for their validity not on themselves nor even solely and exclusively upon consequences (see below on utilitarian ethics). Rather, they appeal for validity to an authority beyond themselves. The morality of human actions is worked out by salvationists primarily by reference to religious criteria.

It is not irrational to speak of ethics depending for validity upon some external authority, despite those who say that this is tantamount to passing the buck of moral responsibility. Ethics is to do with decisions on how to behave and behaviour can flow from a responsibly-taken, prior decision to abide by a moral code which is religious in origin. It is, however, important to identify the authority which it is claimed gives validity to the actions.

Decisions are made by people, not things. Therefore, the authority for Christian ethics must be a person, not a thing, not an office or institution, a custom or tradition. It is common to think in terms of a person who is an authority in ethics. He becomes an authority by being in possession of more data than others and being more practised in using it. In the realm of ethics the data consists of moral facts (which tell us whether an action is right or wrong) as against ordinary facts (which tell us whether a statement is true or false). Whenever we seek advice from another on how to act we are to some extent acknowledging them as an authority. In Christian ethics there is one supreme and final authority.

That authority cannot be the Church since it is not a person but an institution. Neither can we say, without more, that it is the Bible since that is not a person but a book. If the authority we have to identify is a person, could it be a religious leader or the holder of some ecclesiastical office? It appears not, since such a person, despite often great wisdom, is found resorting beyond himself for that wisdom. The basis of Christian ethics and the authority for any act rightly called Christian is the person of Jesus Christ and his

95

teaching. Being divine, he is author of our moral standards: as sinless man, he is also our perfect example. He alone stands before us as our exemplary ideal. Of course, this affords a primary role to Scripture since our knowledge of his life and words is found there and without it we would have no certain guide. But Scripture's role is instrumental. The substance of the revelation is Jesus. He is the content, whilst Scripture is the means.

This then is why we identify Jesus as the authority for all salvationist ethics. No other has discerned truly and responded perfectly to the divine, moral demand that we be complete and mature in God. Only Jesus can claim to have offered the Father total obedience (John 17:4) and only Jesus knows all there is in human nature (John 2:25). Salvationist ethics, like all Christian ethics, is thus Christ-centred. It is captured in phrases like 'following Jesus' and 'the imitation of Christ'. We aim, often failing, to love as he has loved us (John 15:12).

Dietrich Bonhoeffer (*Ethics,* Collins Fontana, 1964) says the same in his inimitable way: 'The only possible object of a Christian ethic (is) an object which lies beyond the ethical, namely the "commandment of God". The commandment of God is something different from . . . the ethical. It embraces the whole of life. It is not only unconditional; it is also total. It does not only forbid and command; it also permits. It does not only bind; it also sets free; and it does this by binding . . . God's commandment is the only warrant for ethical discourse. The commandment of God is the total and concrete claim laid to man by the merciful and holy God *in Jesus Christ*' (italics mine).

It was said above that salvationist ethics do not rely, for their validity, exclusively on the consequences of actions. Full consideration may be given to the consequences of an action, indeed must so be given, and yet the final authority for the action can be elsewhere. This leads us to say that salvationist ethics are not 'utilitarian' ethics. This is less complicated than it sounds. Ever since the work of Jeremy Bentham and J. S. Mill, the utilitarian theory of ethics has continued to exercise a strong influence among moralists down to the present day. In *Utilitarianism* John Stuart Mill (1806-73) defines his principle of 'utility': 'Actions are right in proportion as they tend to promote happiness, wrong as they tend to promote the reverse of happiness.' By happiness he means pleasure and the absence of pain; by unhappiness, pain and the absence of pleasure.

Is there anything of help to Christians in this? To explain a little further, utilitarianism seeks the greatest happiness of the greatest possible number of people. It suggests that pleasure is man's chief goal in life and that it is impossible for a man to act out of any other motive save the pursuit of his own happiness. It brands mankind as inherently and irremediably selfish.

Mill and modern utilitarians tell us that an action is right only if it adds to the sum of happiness in the world. This is a superficially attractive theory, but like so many theories in the study of ethics it needs a second and closer look. It depends entirely upon the idea that a human being cannot desire other than his own personal advantage. Is this true? If it is, then an assertion of the opposite will be self-contradictory. Yet to say 'I desire pain' or 'It is not right in this case to act for the greatest happiness of the greatest number' is not to utter a nonsensical statement. The Christian message is that the power of God can and does re-direct men from selfish and self-centred paths to avenues of generosity and service. Jesus calls us to emulate him in lives of self-sacrificing love. If Mill is right, Jesus is wrong!

Yet it would be a mistake to suggest that utilitarianism is completely invalid. It is not. It rightly stresses that the solution to moral problems should be tied to the diminution of human suffering. At the same time, however, it is far from complete as an ethical theory. Apart from the criticism offered above, these points should be noted:

1 It makes no place at all for the person of Jesus Christ.

2 It does not admit the possibility of there being an authority outside ourselves at whose command or by whose example we should act.

3 Experts have pointed out many loopholes in Mill's account of his own theory. Not the least of these is the notion that we can somehow keep a tally, a credit and debit account, of human pleasures flowing from human actions. He seems to envisage a 'calculus' method of measuring the results of what we do. He wants to base his ethics on the quantity of happiness produced by any given deed, but what place should be given to the quality of happiness? For example, are 10 soccer games better than nine Beethoven symphonies? Who is able to measure the results of human behaviour and to gauge the happiness or pain that we cause? A. D. Lindsay, an expert on the works of Mill, says, 'Only a crude psychology could suppose that pleasures were statable in amounts of each other.' It is true that Mill sees his difficulty here, but he nevertheless sticks firmly to his 'utilitarian' guns.

4 One chief moral concern of the Christian is justice. For this reason too, we have to reject utilitarianism as an adequate ethical system for, whilst it aims to produce as much happiness as possible, it has nothing to say about the distribution of happiness. Justice

would demand a fair distribution of happiness. But utility permits, in fact insists on, anything increasing the happiness of the majority. On this view, the theory requires us to deprive the minority of all happiness if this would increase the happiness of the majority. This is the opposite of justice. As such, it must be abhorrent to those who follow and seek to imitate the Galilean carpenter, the one who befriended the poor and the outcast and who was himself in a minority and still is to this day.

It may be helpful to mention at this point a modern tendency to say, 'There are no moral rules. Take every case as it comes.' This is called 'situation ethics'. Salvationist ethics are not situation ethics. A fashion has sprung up in ethical thinking so that we often hear it claimed that 'what is right' and 'what is expedient' are the same thing, or 'right' means 'useful'. The clearest statement of this approach to morals is found in Joseph Fletcher's *Situation Ethics* (SCM, 1966). This book is well written and readable but certain aspects of it are disturbing.

In brief, situation ethics denies that there are any ethical rules which are universally valid. There are no rules, but there are principles, especially love. So situationism sees itself as a middle way between the two ethical extremes of legalism (sticking rigidly to a pre-fabricated code of rules whatever the consequences) and antinomianism (the view that there are not even principles which need to be followed so that in any given case we can do just as we please).

The situationist accepts only the command to love as being categorically good. But he thinks that this can take an infinite variety of forms and that no absolute rules can be deduced from it. In situation ethics, morality comes down to 'act responsibly in love'. Because of this the situationist will want, as Fletcher puts it, 'to push his principles aside and do the right thing.' He will ignore 'what's right' and do 'what's good'. Fletcher bases his views on 2 Corinthians 3:6: 'The written code kills, the spirit gives life' and also on Galatians 5:14: 'The whole law is fulfilled in one word, "You shall love your neighbour as yourself."' So for the situationist there are no rules, none at all. There are only principles and these are 'advisers without veto power'.

Situation ethics is therefore not a system of ethics. It is rather a 'non-system'. Its approach is pragmatic. It avoids words like 'never', 'always', 'absolutely' when it comes to making a moral choice. It claims that there are no intrinsic values or inherent goods but that moral value attaches to an action only when the action is 'useful'. It does not ask 'What is good?' but rather 'How to do good?' for someone.

What are we to make of all this? An ethic based on love *(agape)* certainly has its attractions for the Christian, and Fletcher rightly stresses the need for proper study of the facts of each situation in which we have to make a moral decision. He is also right to point out the dangers of too legalistic an approach. But the following observations may be made:

1 Situation ethics could easily be seen as merely disguised antinomianism. The theoretical difference between the two is plain enough but the practical differences are hard to see. Fletcher himself speaks of an 'antinomian who lives by a love norm'. It is not easy to see the difference between that and a situationist.

2 The situationist accepts the validity of the biblical injunction to love. Why then does he not accept other biblical injunctions? In what way are they less inspired or less revealed than the '*agape* command'?

3 Can a Christian agree that in every case, or even in any case, 'good' equals 'expedient'? By seeing every situation as an exception and allowing the situation alone to determine one's moral choice, the situationist places at the heart of things the contingent, the casual, the momentary. Can such a view do justice to any idea of final and absolute reality in God?

4 Situationists adopt an approach similar to that of utilitarians but they replace happiness with love so that the aim is to produce the greatest amount of love for the greatest possible number of people. Again, though this is superficially plausible, there are weaknesses to such a 'calculus' view of ethics (see above).

5 There is a logical problem too in saying that it is better to ask 'how' to do good rather than 'what' is good. The logically prior question has to be 'what'. Only when this has been answered can we ask 'how' to put it into effect. It is useless to discuss how a thing ought to be done unless we know what thing it is we are trying to do.

6 By stressing too much the facts of each case, the situationist tends to make our ethics only as effective as our knowledge. Is there not room for God-inspired insight? In making moral decisions the Christian would wish to give greater scope to the gracious influences of God's Spirit, for in the last analysis we are powerless without his grace.

So far, we have not attempted to draw any clear distinction between 'Christian' ethics and 'salvationist' ethics. Clearly, if there is a distinction, it is a fine one, for salvationists, as a distinctive part of God's church, would claim very little indeed for themselves in this field. However, one or two things may be said.

First, not all Christians are agreed on the right answers to the kinds of ethical problems aired briefly in this book. Not even all salvationists share one common view on them. But by and large, the stances taken by the Army (see *Positional Statements,* International Headquarters, 1980) are conservative.

Second, salvationist ethics (as so many think and as sometimes we are capable of encouraging them to think) are not confined just to 'no booze' and 'no baccy'! The total abstention approach, especially to alcohol, goes deep into our fabric as a movement and we counselled on the dangers of using tobacco long before it became respectable so to do. However, our religious convictions lead us to advocate views on a wide variety of issues of modern social concern, far wider than smoking and drinking. The views of the Army on many topics are regularly invited by governments in many parts of the world and almost without exception the invitation is taken up. Salvationist experience, it seems, is deemed of value.

Third, and this is closely linked with the last point, salvationist ethical attitudes are not thought up in an ivory tower but forged on the anvil of innumerable contacts with real people facing life's harsh realities. Their heads are not often in the sand! Salvationists know about human frailty, but they know too about divine power. They know about sin, but also forgiveness. They know spiritual and moral defeat, but also victory in the strength of the Holy Spirit. Hopefully, salvationist ethics are relevant to the lives of ordinary men and women. Ethical positions which bear no relation whatever to the real world are not 'Christian'. So long as salvationist ethics are rooted securely in Christ's gospel, their relevance is assured.

Fourth, if salvationist ethics are applied ethics, that is, having their relevance constantly monitored by the immediacy of human need, they are also 'high-profile' ethics. By this I mean that salvationists are very visible people. Uniforms stand out! The general public, rightly, have high expectations of them, though they are not always able to pass muster. The expectation takes two forms. First, each individual salvationist is under close scrutiny from neighbours and workmates. More will be expected from him in terms of his moral standards than others—and perhaps more even than from other Christians! My grandfather used to work as a foreman in the dockyards at Goole, Yorkshire. He would say, 'Those men expect more of me, as the corps sergeant-major of the local Army corps, than they expect of the anglican vicar!' Every salvationist knows the feeling, knows the pressures. If the salvationist is not different from the rest, he disappoints his Lord, his fellow salvationists and himself—but in a special sense he disappoints those looking on who do not share his beliefs, but respect him for what he is—or claims to be. Second, the public expectation of salvationists in things moral shows itself by the trust exercised by those who come seeking help and counsel. Perhaps more than many religious organisations, we are contacted by or make contact with an entire cross-section of the community. You cannot long be a Salvation Army officer without discovering that human life is varied, amusing, weak, admirable, sordid, confused, confusing, harsh, beautiful and so much more. Those seeking assistance can be old or young, clever or dull, rich or poor, proud or humble, Roman catholic or chapel, believer or atheist. They all come, with expectations high. It takes more than human resources to meet this vast array of need. In many lands, the Army is regarded as belonging to everybody. That is what I mean when I say salvationist ethics, Army stances on things moral and social, are high-profile. The public expectation, in its size and scope, makes it so.

Fifth, when salvationist ethics cease to be imitative of Christ they will cease to be salvationist. It was T. W. Manson who, in explaining 'the imitation of Christ', developed the analogy of the trainee musician who listens to and watches the expert instructor (see his *Ethics and the Gospel,* SCM Press, 1960). In the earliest stages of his training he copies closely the teacher's technique. But, given time and practice, he gradually develops his own style and flair so that the day comes when he can perform creatively whilst nevertheless remaining within the principles and influence of his training. So it is with the imitator of Jesus. As he grows in Christian grace and wisdom he finds himself acting creatively in his moral life yet always remaining true to the example and teaching of his Master.

Salvationists recognise the need for creative, moral reasoning as the world, rich in new knowledge and technology, races ahead of its moral development, bringing new ethical problems. Sometimes Scripture has no 'command of the Lord' and so, as did Paul (1 Corinthians 7:25), we must think for ourselves, asking God's Spirit to teach us all things (John 14:26) and to guide us into all truth (John 16:13).

Helpful reading

Real Questions, David Field and Peter Toon, Lion Publishing, 1982.
The Plain Man's Guide to Ethics, William Barclay, Fontana, 1973.
Christian Ethics and Moral Philosophy, George F. Thomas, Charles Scribner's, 1955.
Ethics and the Gospel, T. W. Manson, SCM Press, 1960.
Ethics and the New Testament, J. L. Houlden, Mowbrays, 1973.
Taking Sides, David Field, Inter-Varsity Press, 1975.